# The Quadrangle
# by Bill Bayles

This book is a conglomeration of short stories about incidents with the interesting and unusual people and characters I have encountered while living and working throughout my life.

While some of the names have been changed to protect the innocent, the events, locales, and characters described in this book are all true to the best of my recollection.

## ACKNOWLEDGMENTS

I have to thank my daughter Diane and her family for their encouragement, support and research in writing and publishing this book.  And thank you to my Grandson, Jacob Melena, for creating the cover.

## DEDICATION

This book is dedicated to my family.

# TABLE OF CONTENTS

## BOOK THREE: ON THE PSYCHIATRIC WARD

## BOOK FOUR: PAROLE AND PROBATION

# Book 1
# CHILDHOOD

## MY VERY FIRST FRIEND

I was two years old when my mother divorced my father, and I never saw him again. After the divorce, she and I went to reside with her best friend Janet.

Janet lived with her parents, Lou and Ralph, who lived above a restaurant they owned and operated in a suburb of Cincinnati, Ohio known as Camp Dennison. My mother earned her room and board for the five of us as a waitress and cleaning lady.

I became fast friends with Ralph's German Shepherd, Caesar, who never left my side. We lived in an area with a majority African American population, most of whom were a bit leery of Caesar, who was big even for German shepherd standards.

I was about four years old when my mother decided she needed help looking after me. She hired Mr. Sisko, a dark skinned man with big, sparkling brown eyes who couldn't have been more than four feet tall. He had no hair or teeth, but he always had a great big ear-to-ear smile. My mother gave Mr. Sisko a dollar a day to keep an eye on me because I had a tendency to wander off.

My mother told me that Mr. Sisko was nearing a hundred years old, and that he'd been born into slavery. He lived near us in a little shack on the Milner Estate with his son Bill. I think they earned their living doing gardening and handyman type work on the property. We were told that the family he worked for had been involved in the Underground Railroad, bringing slaves from the South to the North.

Caesar and I spent most days with Mr. Sisko down by the Little Miami River looking for all sorts of creatures: frogs, tadpoles, salamanders, lizards, snakes, and whatever else we could find. Mr. Sisko once gifted me a garden snake, which I tied a string to and pulled around like a toy.

In the summertime, when the river was warm and shallow, Mr. Sisko would let Caesar and me play in the water. I'd wade in and hold Caesar's collar to keep me afloat. If my mother had found out, she would've fired Mr. Sisko and given me a good spanking.

Mr. Sisko taught me how to fish with a bamboo pole. We used string for fishing line, washers for a sinker, and cork for a bobber. He taught me how to take the fish off the line, and which fish we could eat. When we finished, he would clean and fry what we caught; it always tasted great.

Mr. Sisko would play the harmonica while I fished. He made beautiful music that sounded sad and far off. I guess it was what was popular in the 1930's. He also played gospel or folk music, like "Rock of Ages." There were times when Caesar would begin to howl with the music, which Mr. Sisko called singing.

For my fifth birthday, Mr. Sisko built me a wagon out of scrap wood. Before he could give it to me, however, my real father, Bill Kilius, showed up at my home unannounced and dropped off a shiny new wagon with wooden sides. It was beautiful. When Mr. Sisko brought me his small handmade scrap wagon, I told him I didn't want it because I already had a better one.  My mother was furious when she found out.  I thought I was surely going to get a spanking, "How dare you say that to man who worked so hard to make you a nice gift! Your father owes back child support and doesn't pay it; then he drops off a wagon out of nowhere. I guess he thinks this makes everything right.  You really hurt Mr. Sisko, Billy."

The next day, I went back to Mr. Sisko and told him the brand new wagon was too big for me to handle, so I gave it to Ralph to collect coal that had fallen off the railroad cars.  I think Mr. Sisko appreciated what I did.  And my mother taught me a lesson that I would never forget.

A few months after my birthday, Mr. Sisko died.  He was nicely dressed and laid out in his little shack on top of a table.  That was one of the saddest days of my life.  I loved that little old man, and I will never forget him.

## MY STEPFATHER

When my mother married my stepfather Fred, things looked up.  They got along so well!  They both loved to ride horses, and my stepfather took the time to teach me how to ride and swim.  Once we were out at Coney Island, an amusement park outside of Cincinnati, I was able to swim from there across to Kentucky on the other side, and my mother swam right there with me.  While she was swimming, she lost her wedding ring, but we still had a good time.

My stepfather would buy these "Big Little Books" and he actually taught me how to read.  By the time I started the first grade, I didn't enjoy school at all because the other kids hadn't learned to read yet! It was boring to the end. I spent most of my time looking out the window. I was a quiet student and I didn't cause any problems that I remember, but I think I flunked the first grade. Because I just wouldn't pay attention.

In 1937, my sister Mary Ann was born. We lived in a suburb of Cincinnati that was down by the river. Unfortunately, the flood of 1937 ruined our basement and the first floor of our home, so we had to move.

About two years later, my mother lost a child. I still remember when Fred and I went out back in the woods and buried the baby in a breadbox. My mother blamed the doctor, a man by the name of Reasonback, who convinced her to have the baby at home. She was so upset over the ordeal she never trusted another doctor again.

In 1940, we moved to a place called Green Hills, Ohio, a beautiful settlement built by the government just 30 miles outside of Cleveland. All the houses were nearby to a playground, and my local school had an outdoor pool and hiking trails that led into the woods. I thought I was in heaven! I would have liked to stay there the rest of my life, but unfortunately a few months later my stepfather went into active service and was shipped to Fort Knox, Kentucky.

I still remember my next-door neighbor, Phyllis Williams, and my best buddy Bobby Shangland. Bobby was small for his age and a lot of the kids would pick on him. I'd always have to intervene. My mother and I had a good number of arguments because of all the fights I was getting into, but they were almost always because of Bobby.

One incident in Green Hills stands out particularly well in my mind. When I was 9 years old, we had a paperboy named Red Pennington (who, as I recall, shared a name with the sidekick of the radio program "Don Winslow of the Navy", Don Winslow and Red Pennington). Unlike the radio character, Red was a bully. He especially liked to torment the younger kids in the neighborhood. He would hide behind the above-ground electrical boxes, then jump out, grab us, and knock the wind out of us. Other times, in the swimming pool, he'd dart underneath us and poke us in the groin. Red thought he was hilarious.

When I told my stepfather about all the kids Red had hurt or scared, he just said, "Well, we're gonna have to teach him a lesson." For the next month he taught me judo. He taught me step-by-step what to do when someone grabs you: first, you duck, then grab your assailant's arm, making sure his palm is facing up. Then you position his arm so his elbow is over your shoulder and then pull down as hard as you can. Ideally, you'll flip the assailant right over your shoulder.

At home, my stepfather would hide and then suddenly grab me to see if I remembered to grab his arm with the hand palm up. Occasionally, I was able to flip him! He was pretty quick and we both got a good kick out of it.

After a month of practice, I finally had an opportunity to confront Red. I was walking along the sidewalk when, out of the corner of my eye, I caught him hiding behind an electrical box. I approached the box and slowed down. Sure enough, he jerked out to grab me, palms up. I grabbed his right arm, pulled it up onto my shoulder and yanked as hard as I could. For whatever reason, Red didn't flip, instead, his arm snapped backwards. Shocked, he stepped back and went running down the street. It wasn't long before my mother received a call from Red's, with a story about how I was such a bully and had maliciously broken poor Red's arm.

Now, my mother had a horsewhip that she kept for riding. She was barely off phone before she turned around and gave me the switching of a lifetime. When my stepfather came home, he immediately understood what had happened, "You and Billy come with me. We're going to visit the Pennington's."

The three of us arrived at their home and rang the doorbell. As the door opened, I could see Red sheepishly holding his arm in a cast behind his parents. My stepfather addressed the family, "This is Billy, the boy who broke your son's arm." He went on to explain that it was actually Red terrorizing the other kids in the neighborhood. My mother began to cry as soon as she realized her mistake. She also seemed a bit relieved that I wasn't the bully she thought I was. Later, she baked me an apple pie as an apology, and for the next couple days I had it pretty good.

My stepfather, Fred, told me that there's always going to be a bully like Red, no matter where you go, so you might as well have it out right away. He continued to teach me judo, which I was glad to never have to use again after breaking Red's arm. I never wanted to hurt anyone that badly ever again.

Unfortunately, we didn't stay in Green Hills long. Fred was transferred to Fort Knox, Kentucky, and from that time on, we had to move every six months from one army camp to the next. I found it hard, sometimes impossible, to constantly make new friends, but my stepfather had taught me how to be self-confident, so I never felt inferior even as we moved from one place to the next.

## SHELBYVILLE, TENNESSEE

I really enjoyed Fort Knox, mostly because we lived on base in an actual tent, but my mother wasn't happy. She seemed a little bewildered or depressed that Fred wasn't around very much. It wasn't long before we moved to Shelbyville, Tennessee, where Fred was stationed at Camp Forest. He was on maneuvers, which meant we'd still only see him for two or three weeks at a time. I still liked it, though.

Our school was small and our teacher would read books like "Gulliver's Travels" and "The Wizard of Oz" out loud to us. I never learned anything about grammar, nor did I care to. They also didn't care if I showed up without shoes or a shirt. It was nice for a kid, I suppose. In the summertime, they even had a skating rink on base, and I found out my mother was a phenomenal skater.

Men would flirt with her whenever we went out, which upset me to no end. I said something about it to my stepfather, but he didn't make an issue of it. At the time, my mother was drinking heavily.

Once, she sent me into town to buy beer for her. On the way back, and I ran into soldiers on maneuvers who were not allowed to leave their truck. One of them peered down at me and asked, "Hey kid, what do you got in the bag?"

"Beer, for my mother."

"Toss me one and I'll give you a dollar!" I tossed him a beer, but he only threw back a quarter. The guy next to him said, "Hey, what about me?"

"You throw that dollar out and I'll consider it." It wasn't long before I sold everything I had and made about eight dollars. I ran back to the bar to buy more then turned around and sold those, too. By the time I got home, my mother was furious and gave me a good whipping. My stepfather just sort of laughed and said, "Hey, he's making money, that's great! Don't pick on him." He was always on my side.

Fred's father, who also went by Fred Bayles, frequently came to visit us in Shelbyville. Fred Sr. was a mining engineer. On his visits, he taught me how to play cribbage and told all kinds of stories. He was an interesting man, he told me he once sat on Thomas Edison's lap in a lab in Colorado.

Fred Sr. said that he was a very punctual man who had only ever been late once in his life. Traveling for a routine mine inspection, he missed a train going from New Jersey to West Virginia. By the time he finally reached his destination, he found out that a gas leak had killed everyone inside. It was just fate that he'd been late that day. He would've been dead if he'd made it on time.

# SHIPPED TO CLEVELAND

When I was 10 years old, it seemed that I couldn't please my mother, so she decided to get rid of me for a while. She put me on a Greyhound bus with a note to hand the driver saying my uncle Carl would meet me at the Cleveland bus terminal. She told me I was to go to Cleveland for the summer and that I would live with my grandparents. I didn't enjoy living with grandparents.

My grandfather's name was Otto Lange. Otto was German, and he hated Jews. I remember my grandmother saying to Otto, "How can you hate Jews when Dr. Baer, who owns the house we live in, let's us stay here for free as long as we pay the utilities?" Dr. Baer was a German Jew and one of the nicest people I've ever met. Otto made no comment.

Otto was a member of the German Club, which was three doors down from where we lived. Sometimes my grandmother would send me over to tell Otto that dinner was ready. I remember when I walked in, there was a large photo of Adolf Hitler and a flag with a swastika on it. When Otto would talk to his friends, he would constantly mention Hitler as though he were a great man. Once, he told his friend that Hitler did a great thing by ordering the "parasitic" gypsies to be rounded up and executed. His friend agreed, and acknowledged that they'd be doing the same with the Jews, and the two men laughed. I told my grandmother what I heard, and she said it was the "most evil thing" and that it made her sick.

My grandfather continued to be active in the German Club and praised Hitler until his two sons joined the military service; my uncle Carl joined the Navy, and my uncle Walter joined the Air Force. Given the conflict of interest, the German Club eventually took down their picture of Hitler, and the swastikas. By then the neighborhood had turned on them, and began throwing rocks through their window. The club eventually shut down, and I heard that the people who ran it had disappeared.

Otto was, to his credit, consistent—in that he was always mean and nasty: "Your mother should never have dumped you off on us. She should've put you in an orphanage!" He believed that children should, "be seen but not heard." He would slap me upside the head if he disliked the way I followed his instructions. For example, one evening, when we were eating dinner, I asked my grandmother if I could have the last piece of meat, which nobody seemed to want. She told me I could have it. As I reached for it, my grandfather slapped me and knocked me off my chair.

Walter, my uncle who was only six years older than me, despised Otto even more than I did, which gives you an idea of how bad a man he was. I'd heard that Otto was on disability from an injury he received while working in a factory. After that, he never worked again. He spent the rest of his life drinking beer with his buddies and playing cards at a local bar. Supposedly, he was a very good gin player and always had money on him, but he never offered to give my grandmother money to help with her household expenses.

# MY GRANDMOTHER

As mean as my grandfather was, my grandmother was the opposite; warm and kind. She actually made a living taking care of a half dozen elderly people who were younger than she was.  As a Seventh Day Adventist, she was always trying to save somebody's soul.  I remember she came to me one day and was very upset because her next-door neighbor, Mrs. Knapp, was not very friendly.  She said, "Every time I go outside and hang clothes or something, she runs into her house as though she doesn't want to speak to me."  I told her, "Gran, Mrs. Knapp is a devout Catholic, and you are always trying to convert her to your religion.  For God's sake, if anyone is going to heaven, it is Mrs. Knapp. She is a very nice person and she goes to church three or four times a week. What more can the lord ask?"  My grandmother sighed lightly and said, "Well Billy, maybe you are right." From that point on, they got along.

I feel compelled to talk about my grandmother because I loved her and because she was such a compassionate person. She had no formal education. She grew up in Germany, and taught herself how to read and write. She could speak three or four languages. She really was an amazing lady.

There were times when my grandmother had members of the Church over to the house. They would all gather around a table and my grandmother would ask me to read from the bible. I would start reading, and they would begin to recite it ahead of me. I once stopped to ask,

"Why are you having me read it when you have it memorized?"

"We just love to hear you read, Billy!" Really though, I think they believed that having me read from the bible would have a positive effect on me. Maybe they were right. Who knows?

My grandmother was very secretive about her age. In fact, if I called her "Grandma" in the store, she would run away from me, and say, "Don't call me Grandma!" I asked her one time how old she was and she told me. I said, "If you are really that old, you must've had my mother when you were four years old." She didn't reply; she didn't want to talk about it.

I remember when I was nine or ten, I would go caroling with my grandmother and other members of the Church. They had a band and we would collect money for the needy. I always believed that the money we collected went to help needy people all around the world. I did well collecting money because I'd go into bars and I got more money in 15 minutes than the others would get going house to house in the whole neighborhood.

The first evening we went caroling, I started to get cold so I stopped in the entranceway of a bar. When one of the women who was either a waitress or the owner's wife (or both) said to me, "What are you doing out here this late at night in this cold weather?" She took me inside and yelled to the patrons, "This little boy is out caroling in this cold weather to raise money for the needy people around the world. Let's pitch in and make a contribution to his cause." She passed the can around to the customers and they filled it to a point where I couldn't put any more money in it.  Then she gave me a dollar and said it was only for me.  I was elated and, when I showed my grandmother how much money I collected, she laughed and said I had collected more money than all the other people in the group.  I never told her that I'd collected the money from a bar, or I might have ended up with a spanking.  But from then on, every time I went caroling I made a point of stopping in and soliciting the neighborhood bars.  When we got home, my grandmother told Otto that I collected more money than all the rest of the group.  Otto's only comment was, "How much did he steal?"  My grand mother told him, "Stop picking on Billy, you're just being ridiculous!"

One afternoon, my grandmother received a letter asking her to meet with the principal of Sackett grade school.  The letter said that I was failing and the principal would like to talk to us after school.  The principal told my grandmother that I was failing and, if there were no changes for the better, I would not be promoted to the next grade level.

My grandmother asked the principal, "Is this because Billy's not behaving in class?"  The principal said, "No, Billy is very quiet and spends most of his time looking out the window.  He doesn't pay attention in class and never completes his homework.  My grandmother said she had talked to her son Carl and that Carl would sit down with Billy and make sure he completes his homework.  He would also ask Billy what he learned in class each day so, hopefully, Billy will listen in class.  The principal told my grandmother that she was very satisfied with their meeting.

Unfortunately, my grandfather Otto had seen and read the principal's letter. He told me, "You're just a worthless dummy and you'll never amount to nothing! That's why your mother dumped you off on us!"

I was thankful that my uncle Carl sat down with me every night and made sure that I completed my homework. Carl also said he'd take me fishing if I was promoted to the next level. Carl kept his word; he took me camping and fishing the next weekend. Carl was drafted into the Navy and shipped to Chicago to the Great Lakes boot camp. I didn't see him for a number of years. He was a good friend and I knew I would miss him. After that, I went back to looking out the window at school.

## MY FIRST REAL JOB

I loved my grandmother, but I had one problem with her: she didn't believe in going to the movies. As a Seventh Day Adventist, she thought it was a sin. One of the few things I enjoyed doing with my mother was going to the movies, and I suppose I missed it.

Eventually, I found a way to make money as a stock boy and cleaner at Helms Drugstore. I worked Sunday through Thursday. My grandmother wouldn't allow me to work Fridays or Saturdays, she believed the Sabbath was from Friday sundown to Saturday sundown, and parishioners were not supposed to work on the Sabbath.

One Saturday afternoon, I decided to use my proceeds to go see a movie with two of my buddies: "Gunga Din", a 19th century adventure film about three British soldiers and a water bearer named Gunga Din. I was so fascinated by the film that I went back to watch it four more times that day. When I finally got home, it was well past 11 PM. That was the only time my grandmother ever spanked me, and I wasn't even upset because I knew I deserved it. When Otto found out, he declared, "We should put Billy in the Jones Home Orphanage." I was mortified, the children from there attended the same school I did, and I felt sorry for them. They had these terrible haircuts and clothes that looked like they'd been worn too many times. They seemed so unhappy.

I came into the drugstore the next day, and Mr. Helms saw that I was pretty depressed. He asked me what was wrong, so I told him about Otto's threat to send me away. Mr. Helms knew my grandfather, "That man's an old crab. Maybe I can help you out." He gave me a carton of Lucky Strike cigarettes, the same brand that Otto liked. At the time, cigarettes were being rationed because they were being sent to the US soldiers overseas. Mr. Helms smiled and said, "Your grandfather will be grateful and hopefully, he'll treat you a little better!"

I walked home with the cigarettes in hand, triumphant, and immediately gave them to Otto as a peace offering. He took them, inspected them for a moment, and then threw them at my feet, "You're either going to reform school or to an orphanage!"

When I told my grandmother, she walked with me to speak with Mr. Helms, who explained to her that he'd given me the cigarettes in the hopes that Otto would treat me better. Back home, my grandmother tried to explain the situation to Otto. He only grunted, "Mr. Helms is an old fool and Billy is probably stealing from him."

I felt sick. I loved Mr. Helms. He'd lost his only son at the start of World War II, and I often caught him crying in the back room. I hated my grandfather for calling him a fool.

## DROWNING IN BROOKSIDE

Now that my grandmother was friends' with Mrs. Knapp, I began to spend some time with her son Jimmy, who was around my age. We decided to go to Brookside Park to go swimming. It was a beautiful day and Jimmy decided to swim a bit further out than he'd ever had before, into the deep end. I wasn't paying much attention until I heard a splash, and then saw his head dip under the surface. I dove under the water and tried to pull him out, but he was too heavy. Panicking, I called to a lifeguard but she just stood there, unsure what to do. Some high school boys heard me yelling, and they helped me drag Jimmy out after I pulled him up as far as I could. We paddled Jimmy out all the way to the shoreline, and laid him on the ground. He was blue and not breathing, but the older boy's were able to revive him.

A local newspaper heard about the incident, and they put my name in the paper. A little article mentioned that my stepfather was in the army and I remember being so proud that I brought it home to show Otto. But he didn't bother to read it.

I still have the article.

## Boy Risks His Life to Save
## Chum From Death in Pool

*James Knapp & Billy Bayles*

*Youth isn't apt to ponder too much over what might have been, but the bond of friendship between Jimmie Knapp, 13, and Billy Bayles, 11, both of 3240 W. 25th Street, was immeasurably tighter today. Jimmie would have drown yesterday in Brookside Park pool had it not been for his chum.*

*Jimmie, still in the paddling stage, speedily got into trouble when he sought to swim to a diving board.*

*Billy, more proficient, saw him struggling and went to is rescue his rescue but was scratched and clawed by the other, in an unreasoning panic. He screamed for help but the crowd on shore, including a woman life-guard, thought it was merely horse-play and no body responded.*

*Frantically swimming to shore, Billy finally attracted the attention of two older boys who jumped in, pulled Jimmie out and revived him by artificial respiration.*

*In the excitement they disappeared without giving their names, leaving the police to complete the job by taking Jimmie to City Hospital, where he was discharged after an hour's observation.*

*Jimmie and Billy were out playing together today but their adventures, they promised each other, will not include swimming. There was be one interlude in their play, however.*

*Billy had a letter to write. It was to be penned to his dad, Lieutenant Fred Bayles, at Camp Belvoir, Va., who will be proud to learn that his son can take care of situations on the home-front.*

## FOUR COUSINS IN TROUBLE

Occasionally, my three cousins Tommy, Johnny, and Carl would come to visit me, which was a nice reprieve from my grandparents. I considered myself a sort of daredevil. When my cousins and I were together, we'd perform stunts like walking along the edge of a 100 foot high bridge. Once, we went jumping roofs and my cousin Johnny actually crashed through into a neighbor's garage below. We pretended that we were up there looking for a kitten, but of course I ended up in trouble with my grandfather later.

The first time I was able to leave and visit my cousins, who lived in East Cleveland, we went to a movie theater called the Ambassador, at 125th and Superior Avenue in Cleveland. My Aunt Dolly gave us each a quarter: 10 cents for the movie, 15 cents for candy and popcorn. There was a double feature that night, plus a cartoon, a newsreel, and a serial (which was an ongoing story that ran for several weeks). That particular Sunday, they had a special event: a pretty young girl, a teenage boy, and an elderly man who were all yo-yo champions came to put on a demonstration with their yo-yos. After the demonstration, the audience was told that there would be a yo-yo contest next Saturday. There would be beautiful prizes and there would be five different age divisions and all girls and boys were invited.

The following week, we were out of money, but we had a plan to go into the five and dime and steal some candy. I came up with the idea that we could stash candy in our pants if we cut pockets in our knickers (which had a tight elastic band just under the knee). The candy would fall down and pool at our knees.

I think we would have made it out of the store if Tommy hadn't decided to steal some yo-yos so that we could compete in the yo-yo contest that coming Saturday. Tommy was so skinny that the band on the leg of his knickers wasn't tight against his leg; when he started to walk out of the store, four yo-yos fell out of his pants and bounced off the floor. The manager caught us and called my uncle Joe, who was Carl's father. When we got home, uncle Joe took us all down to the basement. He brought out a switch, which consisted of four thin branches of a sycamore tree. Uncle Joe said, "I'm going to teach you boys a lesson so you'll never steal again!" He made us drop our pants and gave us each ten lashes that left bright red marks on our behinds.

Some months later, Joe's wife, my Aunt Dolly, asked me, "Don't you think Joe was a little cruel and brutal giving you boys such a beating?" I replied dryly, "The only thing I know is, I don't think any of us are going to steal again."

When my grandfather found out about the incident, he declared, "Billy belongs in a detention home for boys that don't know how to behave."


## CAR SLEDDING

One weekend, my cousins came over to stay at my grandparents' house for the weekend. There was such heavy snow that the schools had closed, so we had a lot of downtime to play outside. Friday, I learned that my cousins had never been "car sledding." Trying to show off, I decided I'd show them how. When a car stopped at a stop sign, we would grab onto the back bumper and ride down the street. We were having a lot of fun until my

24

glove got caught in one of the bumpers. I frantically tried to free myself as the car dragged me onto a main street which had been plowed clear of snow. The clean road ripped up my pants and scraped my leg quite badly until I was finally able to squirm free. Back at the house, my grandmother rushed me to Dr. Baer's office so he could treat my leg.

My three cousins were spanked and, of course, it was my fault. Otto looked at me with disdain, "You cause us nothing but trouble! That's why your mother doesn't want you…and we sure don't want you! You're nothing but a pain in the ass!"

## A DANGEROUS INTERACTION

I met Sonny at Gambles Bowling Alley while I was playing on a pinball machine. Sonny, a kid who looked about my age, walked up and asked me if I could show him how to use the machine and hit a high score without tilting or "cheating." We quickly became friends and we would meet every Saturday afternoon, eat lunch, and play the machines.

Sonny worked Saturdays for his uncle who owned Kaufman's Furniture, which was located almost across the street from where my grandmother lived. Sonny washed the windows, vacuumed, dusted, and then, in the evening, he would close up the store by setting the alarms.

One Saturday afternoon, my aunts and uncles were coming to visit, and I decided to bring Sonny over to meet them. One of my uncles brought a Ouija board for the group of adults to play. I'd never seen my grandmother so upset! She took one look at it and gasped, "Those are the work of the devil!" She was so upset she got up and walked out of the house, "I'll return when you get that thing out of my house."

Sonny and I watched my aunts and uncles play with the board. It was strange to see adults asking a piece of wood real questions, expecting real answers.

My grandmother finally returned to the house after they'd left. They had forgotten to take the Ouija board with them. My grandmother, aghast, grabbed it and hauled it to the backyard, poured kerosene on it, and burned it. Both Sonny and I agreed that my grandmother genuinely believed the Ouija board had some connection to the devil.

Sonny told me that he had to leave to go over to the furniture store, so I went with him. He showed me how he set the alarms. There were a dozen wires set six inches off the floor in the aisles. The wires were attached to an alarm switch that would alert the police if an intruder stepped on a wire or if his leg pulled one out of the wall. He said all the windows had alarms on them except for a small window in the store's bathroom, which was so high off the ground that no one could get in, anyway.

When Sonny's uncle was ready to close up shop, I noticed his uncle removed the money from the cash register and placed it in a small box, which he set on a shelf in his office. I told Sonny I thought it was unusual that he would put the money in a box instead of in a safe, which is what Mr. Helms did to deter theft. In the morning when Mr. Helms opened the store, he would just take the money out and place it back in the register. Sonny said they had a safe in the furniture store, and he couldn't figure out why his uncle didn't use it.

A few months passed, and I decided that I was sick of being mistreated by my grandfather. I hatched a plan to run away and see my mother, sister, and stepfather in Maryland. I remembered where Mr. Kaufman would store the money-box after hours. Sonny said Saturdays were the best day of the week in the furniture business, I decided I was going to take the money and use it to safely make my way to Maryland. I figured Mr. Kaufman was a rich man and would not miss a little bit of money.

So, on a Saturday when Sonny was not working (I did not want his uncle to think Sonny took the money), I snuck into the furniture store just before closing and I hid in the basement. After the store was closed and everybody was gone, I carefully stepped up the stairs, being very careful not to step on the alarm wires. When I got to Mr. Kaufman's office I found the stash of money and took it all except for the change. Satisfied, I went to the store's bathroom and opened the small window. I looked out in the alley; there was no one in the area, so all I had to do was hang out the window and drop down six feet to the ground. Then I'd be home safe.

But a thought came to me and I started to feel sick. My Nazi grandfather was right about me: I was just a thief who should be in jail. I couldn't stand the thought that he was right about me. I spun around and walked right back to Mr. Kaufman's office. I placed the money in the box, but did not return the box to the shelf. I left it in on his desk. I thought maybe Mr. Kaufman would learn a lesson; that he should start using his safe. I went back to the bathroom, dropped out of the window to the ground, and walked home. I had almost made a terrible mistake.

## A GREYHOUND BUS TRIP

I was still determined to escape my grandfather. I was sick of fighting with him, and I missed my family. I talked Mr. Helms' daughter into buying me a Greyhound bus ticket to Washington, DC. I told her I was just going to be there for the weekend. In case anyone bothered me, I forged a note from my grandmother saying that my mother would meet me at the bus terminal in Washington. Instead, when I reached Washington, I had enough money to take a cab to Cover Manor, Maryland, where my mother lived.

I showed up at her house and knocked. I was so happy to have finally made it. My mother opened the door, but she wasn't pleased to see me, "What do you think you're doing here?" She yanked me into her home by my hand, "My dad is right, you're nothing but trouble!" I was heartbroken. She phoned my grandmother, "You can stop worrying. The brat is here."

She didn't, however, immediately send me back. We only lived in Cover Manor for only a short time before we moved to Washington, DC. We briefly lived in an apartment in which turned out to be infested with rats. My stepfather was on leave, and he found us a place in Alexandria, VA, where the four of us lived for a bit on Palatine Road.

It was the beginning of the summer in Alexandria, and I was fortunate to find a job delivering papers in the morning. I had a large route, with 230 papers, and I earned a cent and a half on each paper plus 5 cents on the Sunday paper. I had a ton of spending money; the only downside being I had to wake up at 5 AM, and I had to compete with a 16 year old boy named Junior, who had a similar route.

Because of the war, my stepfather left often to go overseas. The more he was away, the more my mother drank. There was always a pattern to her drinking: the first day he was away, she'd drink wine until she was obnoxious and violent. The second day she'd be hung-over and quiet. The third day she was normal and pleasant to be around, and on the fourth day the cycle would repeat itself.

Once, she caught me trying to dilute her wine with water. She threw an ashtray at my head; thank God it missed me. It stuck in the wall behind me, I think it would have killed me.

We were still living in Alexandria come winter of that year. My mother stepped out of her house to go shopping one day when she slipped on some ice and broke her arm. Our neighbor rushed her to the Walter Reed Hospital in Washington, D.C, where a doctor accidentally put a cast on too tight, constricting the blood flow to her tendons, ligaments, and nerves in her arm. A series of botched operations left her arm shriveled up and about one-fifth the size of a normal arm. She had to remain in the hospital for several months.

My stepfather was overseas in Burma and couldn't return home until April of that year. A neighbor helped looked after my sister Mary Ann and me during that time. Mary Ann and I would either go over to her house to eat, or our neighbor would cook food and bring it over to us. Our neighbor did the best she could.

## SKIPPED SCHOOL

From September to April, while my mother was in the hospital and while my stepfather was abroad, I stopped going to school. When he returned, I explained to him that I tried to enroll, but couldn't because I didn't have a transcript from my previous school. I expected my stepfather to be mad at me, but he just said, "You probably got quite an education these past couple months." Fred managed to convince the administration to enroll me in the last month of school. Afterwards, they gave me a handwritten letter stating that, due to poor attendance, I would have to repeat the 7th grade.

The following school year we would move to Cincinnati, Ohio, and I changed the "7" in my letter to an "8," so that I wouldn't be held back. Thus, I started school in Cincinnati in the 8th grade. I thought I was being clever, but it affected my education and gave me a lot of problems down the road.

By the end of the summer, my mother was released from Walter Reed. She hadn't been drinking while in the hospital, but her shriveled arm made it impossible for her to go out of the house unless she had a few drinks in her. The situation created a lot of problems for the rest of us.

# BILLY'S PAPER ROUTE

I had quite the paper route in Alexandria. It covered a beautiful stretch of land near the Potomac River. An African American population lived in houseboats along the water. I delivered their papers and a few folks let me fish right off their boats. I couldn't clean or cook the fish, so I always gave the owners whatever I caught. I just loved to fish.

I delivered a paper to two elderly women who owned a cow named Daisy that needed to be milked twice a day. The ladies said that if I would milk the cow in the morning, I could keep the milk. I liked helping the two ladies. I hated the milk, however, so I gave it to the people who owned the riverboats. They said it was perfect for their coffee.

I also delivered papers to a man named John L. Lewis, the head of the United Mine Workers. One day, he chewed me out for leaving his paper in the rain. I apologized, and, from then on, I put his paper inside the screen door of his house. At the end of the month when I went to collect for the papers, his housekeeper paid me for the month and also gave me a five-dollar tip, which was the biggest tip I had ever received while delivering papers.

One day, Ray, the paper route manager, told me they were having a special deal for newspaper boys. He said, if you get 25 new subscriptions to the paper, you'd win a one-day boat trip on the Chesapeake Bay along with two meals, plus a lot of other prizes. I was able to get ten new subscriptions on my route. I asked Ray where I could go to pick up 15 more subscriptions. He told me, "Well,

Junior never tried to get any new subscriptions along his route, so you should go to Junior's area. Junior won't mind because it'd mean more money for him when he goes on his route." Within three days, I picked up the subscriptions I needed and won the Chesapeake Bay trip.

When Junior found out what I'd done, he was furious. We happened to both deliver papers to the same apartment building, and he caught me as I was trying to drop off a paper. "I didn't give you permission to go into MY route!" He smacked me with his canvas sack of newspapers, scraping my skin. He hit me again, and again, until I was bleeding. A custodian saw what was happening and grabbed the sack from Junior.

The custodian apparently told Ray what he'd seen. I'm not sure what transpired between Junior and our manager, but a few days later I found out that Junior would be taking over my route. I was to be promoted, and take over Mike Athens' route, a guy who had just graduated high school and left to join the US Army. Mike had 300 papers to delivery everyday. It was an easy route because his papers came bundled together and I could just drop off a bundle on the first floor of each apartment building I stopped at. Most of the people on Mike's route paid by mail, which meant I didn't have to collect money in person. Instead of making 50 cents a day, I started making $3 a day.

The problem I had on that route was when I needed to collect money from people who were moving out in the middle of the month. I started offering building managers a free paper if they would let me know if anyone was moving out in the middle of the month. That way, I could go and collect before someone skipped out on a payment.

Occasionally, someone would give me a hard time when I tried to collect early, but I would insist, "My father is an officer in the Army. He won't like to hear that you're cheating out a little kid." That line always worked.

Despite the perks, I missed my old paper route because I seldom saw any of the people I used to deliver to along the river. In fact, I rarely interacted with anyone on Mike's route, except the ones I had to collect from at the end of the month.

## ONE OF THE SADDEST DAYS IN MY LIFE

One of the saddest days in my life happened in Alexandria, VA. I came home one afternoon to find my mother in a foul mood and smelling of wine. I knew the best thing for me to do was to stay out of her way. I went to my room to figure out what I owed Ray from the money I had collected that month.

But when I opened my cashbox, all the money was gone. The money I owed for the papers, plus my profit. I went to my mother and asked her if she'd taken my money.

"Yes, Fred's monthly check hasn't come in yet."

"Is there any left? Most of that money isn't mine." I pleaded with her, but she didn't seem to understand what I was even saying.

"Look, there's some left, but I need it."

"All you need that money for is wine!" I started to look around for where she'd set Ray's money down, when my mother grabbed her horsewhip. She started to whip me, but she was so drunk that it was easy for me to grab it from her, "You're not going to beat me. This is wrong." She screamed and began calling me names until she stormed out of the house. An hour later, she returned, still drunk: "You think you're so tough fighting with your crippled mother. Well, there are some boys outside that are going to give you the beating you deserve." I looked outside and saw about six high-school students standing on our front walk, waiting for me. Frustrated and angry, I ran outside kicking, screaming, and punching.

But instead of beating me, the boys scooped me up and carried me away to their friend's house. Inside, one of them handed me a coke. "I couldn't believe your mother would pay someone to beat you up." I was shocked. They told me to stay away from her until she sobered up. I knew the money the boys had was mine, but I didn't ask for it and they didn't offer to return it. So, the money was gone.

The next morning, after I'd delivered my papers, I went to Ray's house and explained to him and his wife what had happened. They were very sympathetic, and both agreed that we should let it go until my stepfather came home. Ray said, "If we go over and try to get your money back, it's going to cause more problems. Your mother might not even remember what happened last night."

## A DOG NAMED DUKE

One morning, at about 5 AM when I was on my way to deliver my newspapers, I heard a dog bark. I looked around until I saw a large, jet-black German shepherd behind a fence. He immediately reminded me of Caesar, the dog I loved when I was four. The dog appeared to be guarding the back of a liquor store in plain sight I could see cases of beer, wine, and other alcohol in an open garage. As I approached, he started to growl and gnash his teeth. I thought he was beautiful: "You and I are going to be friends."

The next day, I found out the dog's name was Duke. I brought him a pack of hot dogs, which I cut into four pieces. I pushed the food through the fence and encouraged him to eat. A few weeks later, Duke was eating out of my hand.

One morning, Duke didn't jump up when he saw me. He had a long chain hooked around his leather collar that tethered him to his doghouse. The chain had somehow wrapped itself around his back leg; without thinking, I opened the gate and unhooked it off his leg. That was the first time I'd actually approached him. After that, I would go inside and sit with him whenever I fed him. I never touched the merchandise because I wasn't sure how Duke would react, but I loved to sit and pet him.

A few weeks later, on a Sunday afternoon, two high school students were kicking a football around near Duke's fence. One of the boys accidentally kicked the ball into the fenced area that Duke was guarding. As they approached, the dog growled and they backed off. I think they were going to wait until Monday to retrieve their ball, but as soon as I heard what had happened I walked over and told them that Duke was a friend of mine, "Wait here. Stand on the other side of the street so you don't upset him."

I walked over to the enclosure and told Duke, "I'm just going to get the ball." Duke watched me as I slipped inside, picked up the ball, and walked out. He never moved an inch. The boys thanked me for retrieving their ball, and one commented, "I didn't think that dog had any friends."

A few days later, Duke's owner came to our house to tell my mother that he had a problem with me. The father of the boy whose ball I retrieved had apparently told him that I'd gone into Duke's pen. Duke's owner told us, "I spent a lot of money ordering that dog from Germany, where he was trained as a guard dog. If anyone tried to get in, he would be attacked and maybe killed. So, what happened?" My mother turned to me and asked me, "Billy, did you go into Duke's pen?"

"Yes, but the dog had a chain wrapped around his leg and couldn't move." The owner seemed to buy my story, and I had to promise my mother that I'd never go inside Duke's pen again. I promised, but I continued to see Duke every morning I could until I left Alexandria.

## THE WORLD OF MIRTH

For one week in the middle of the summer, The World of Mirth Carnival came to Alexandria. They travelled with at least thirty trailers, each with big beautiful signs on their sides advertising different aspects of the carnival. It took two days for them to set up the carnival with all the rides, tents, and booths. I was fascinated, and after asking around I was able to get a job as a cleanup guy.  I carried a stick with a nail on the end, and I'd pick up rubbish.

The carnival was open from 12 noon until 12 midnight, except on Saturdays and Sundays when it stayed open until 1 AM.  A large PA system played music that could be heard throughout.  There were several large tents, each colorfully striped.  The sides of the tents had pictures of whatever attraction was inside the tent.  There were rides tucked away in different corners: a Ferris wheel that spun around so fast it would make me sick, bumper cars, two different merry-go-rounds, and more.  My favorite ride was a swing that you'd get strapped into and swing around very fast.  It was all so new and exciting.

At night, they pointed floodlights into the sky as to attract customers from all over.  There were lights and streamers all over the carnival, and they had hired off-duty police to patrol and keep order.

There were about twenty or so booths that challenged customers to different carnival games.  You could try to extinguish candles with a squirt gun, knock dolls over with a baseball, or swing a hammer to determine how strong you were.  There was even a booth where a man would guess your weight.  If he wasn't within five pounds, you would win a doll.  The most popular stand was a clown sitting in a chair over a barrel of water where you threw a ball at a target, and the clown would be dunked if you hit a bulls-eye. Off-duty clowns would walk around and sell balloons and other merchandise to customers.

The largest tent they had was the "penny arcade," which probably had about a hundred machines, all you needed was a penny. The second largest tent was a staff tent, where the carnival staff would lounge and eat. They had several cooks cooking for the staff almost all day. For the guests, there was everything you could imagine, from cotton candy, hot dogs, taffy, ice cream, and a lot more.

The other large tents were designated for the slideshow attractions. "Barkers" with megaphones would announce which attractions were happening when. They had a variety of shows: There was "the strongest man in the world", performing great feats of strength. The man looked like a Sumo wrestler. I once tried to lift one of his weights and I couldn't even get it to budge. The carnival also had a woman who they claimed to have the largest head in the world. She was a young lady, with a head that sure enough was several times the size of a normal adult. I later realized that she was hydrocephalic, and I felt sorry that she was put on display. They also had "The Elephant Man", who looked like he had grey plaster all over his body (which might've actually been the case). There were dancing girls, unfortunately none of whom were very pretty, and a gypsy fortuneteller (who sometimes performed as "the Tattooed Lady"). My favorite act was the "Performing Dogs." A woman with eight highly trained terriers had them perform tricks and coordinated stunts. There were many other shows: there was a group of black children who sang and danced, the youngest being about 4 and the oldest was around 12. Some of the children belonged to the tattooed lady, and the others belonged to other staff members.

The most disturbing slideshow was "The Cobra Lady." Inside one of the larger tents there was a 30 foot long pit about 4 feet deep, with a canvas on the floor. In the middle sat a crippled woman with horribly deformed arms. Her skin was sallow, and hung off her face like dripping wax. In her whole mouth she only had two teeth, both broken and green. Her hair was filthy and matted. She was surrounded by about sixty snakes, crawling around her, ranging from cobras to rattlers. A big sign said, "please do not throw pennies in the pit. Silver is ok." She would pull live mice from the folds of her clothes and feed them to the snakes whenever spectators threw nickels and dimes down at her. An employee informed me that these snakes had their venom sacs cut so that their bite wouldn't kill someone (instead, a victim would only get a bad infection). It was a sickening sight.

There were gypsies in the Carnival, too, who mostly kept to themselves, and played music near their caravan. While I was there, one of them was once accused of theft. The owner and the manager of the carnival searched their trailer for any stolen goods, but nothing was found.

I became friends with one of the gypsies children, a boy who I called "Sabu" (because he looked like Sabu from the "Jungle Book"). Sabu told me about the people who worked at the carnival. I was surprised to find out that almost everyone at the carnival had more than one job. Setting up and taking down the tents was a shared responsibility for everyone who was able. The fattest lady in the world ran the kitchen and did the cooking. The "strongest man in the world" was an Olympic weightlifter, with medals to prove it, but also a mechanic. The knife thrower was also an artist who did portrait drawings. His assistant (who was also his wife), ran the dog show. The bearded lady lived with his wife in a trailer, and they worked doing electrical repairs and replacing lights. The dancers helped in the other acts and worked in the kitchen. The fortuneteller sewed and repaired the tents and costumes; her husband watched the children.

The Carnival also had six semi trucks, a gas truck, and a number of other miscellaneous trailers that were pulled by a pickup truck. A man by the name of Joe Marn was the acting mechanic, and when we were stationary, he often had time to chat with me. I asked him about the strange sideshow attraction, the Cobra Lady. Joe sighed, and said, "You might not believe it, but years ago she was beautiful. She performed as a dancer and for her signature act she'd dance holding a giant python."

Everything I learned about the carnival seemed to add to the appeal and mystery. Eventually, they picked up and moved to Tacoma Park, Maryland. I was so fascinated that I followed them to Tacoma. I was seriously considering running away to join.

In Tacoma, I was showing off when I threw a handful of pennies into the Cobra Lady's pit. They landed in her lap. Her neck jerked up to lock eyes with me and she screamed. I've never seen a look of such hatred, she seemed to look right through me. She began to throw snakes off her body and right out of the pit. She was more agile than I thought possible, she sprang herself up and over the edge of the pen and grabbed my arm as I tried to run. Her nails were long and turned under like an animal's claw, they dug into me so badly I thought I would need stitches. Two attendants came to drag her away.

Sabu brought me to his mother, the Tattooed Lady. She cleaned and bandaged my arm, and sat me down, "You must never make fun of people who are physically deformed or mentally ill. If you do, one day, you'll be afflicted that way, too."

I was still a bit in shock when Joe Marn came to me. "I didn't finish telling you about the Cobra Lady. In her later years, she became an alcoholic. She developed rheumatoid arthritis which gives her tremendous amounts of pain. The more she drank, the more the joints in her hands and legs became shriveled, deformed, and twisted. She lost her teeth, and there was a point when it seemed like she'd do anything for a drink." I felt terrible. Joe kept going, "She was always a good person. Carnival life was the only thing she knew and loved. She became the snake lady. I think the carnival owner should have put her in a home, but she was still bringing in money."

I knew I was wrong for throwing pennies at her. Not long before, I had wanted to leave home to join the carnival, but it no longer had the same appeal to me. It felt wrong to make fun of people who were handicapped. After I left, I had nightmares about the look she'd given me, the hatred in her eyes. I had it coming, I suppose.

## FROM VIRGINIA TO CINCINNATI

Moving to Cincinnati was a very big change for me. I called my stepfather's parents Gram and Gramp. My first impression of them was what I called "high society" ;they were very good people, well-educated, but very regimented.

There were times when I felt like an embarrassment to my grandmother. She constantly corrected my grammar and encouraged me to continue my education. In fact, if it wasn't for her and my grandfather, I probably would have quit school by the time I was sixteen.

My grandmother would always bring me to the grocery store to help her, and she was very picky about what we ate. I think she was so regimented about our eating because my grandfather was diabetic.

My grandmother, however, did smoke; but because it was during the war, she smoked out of a corncob pipe. I thought this was completely out of character, but she loved to smoke and work on crossword puzzles. The day she died, she was doing just that. She passed peacefully; my grandfather even turned to her and warned her she was going to burn her hand, but at that point she had already passed. That's the way to go, I think. Doing what you love.

My grandfather and I talked often. He would tell me about his life and experiences, just like when he visited us in Shelbyville, Tennessee. He was a man who would catalog everything. Everything had a place. He would save his ties because he said that they would come in and out of style and he was not interested in continually buying new ties. He was neat and orderly, that's for sure. We played a lot of cribbage together and he loved to smoke a cigar. He had maybe one or two beers with my mother, but then he told her he stopped drinking.

Their home was located at 292 McGregor Avenue in a little village called Mount Auburn, which was only a couple of blocks from the William Harding Taft home.

They were Episcopalians, people of high moral standards. I understood that they were somewhat disappointed in my stepfather when he chose a career in the army. He had been going to the University of Cincinnati to study pharmacy, and could have breezed through it because he was a very intelligent man. But that just wasn't what he was interested in.

My best friend in Cincinnati was Harry Goebel. I spent more time at his house than I did at Gram and Gramps. Harry's mother was like a mother to me. When she caught Harry and me skipping school one time, she said to me, "You can take ten swats like Harry or we can go over to your grandparents and let them know you are skipping school." I was glad to take the ten swats from her.

Since Harry was a year older than me, his mother would give me his hand-me-down clothes, all of them nice, beautiful things. She told me that I'd have to go to church with them and even enrolled me in the Nash Memorial Methodist Church that was in downtown Cincinnati. She was always looking after me and I really loved her.

The Nash Memorial Church was the first time I became involved in a Sunday school program. The teacher, whom we called Mr. B (for Barringer), had a lot of influence on young people, which kept us coming back to Sunday school and kept a good group of people in the class. Plus, if you wanted to play on the Sunday school team, you had to attend Sunday school at least twice a month.

Another family that Harry and I were close to, the Holly family, lived on the same street that I did with Gram and Gramp. Bud Holly was a pianist, and had a beautiful sister who was married to a bandleader. I also remember their older brother Charles, and sister Carol. June, our closest friend of the Holly's, was our age and in eighth grade with us, so we spent a lot of time at their house. Their mother was always a good hostess and treated us like part of the family.

I had other good friends in Cincinnati, too. Bill Pangborn lived a couple of blocks away. Bill Stapleton was in my class at William Howard Taft. Then there was Glen Ward and another buddy of Bill's named Howard Parrot. Howard died in the Korean War. I remember him as pretty wild.

On Saturdays, I worked with Harry at the Covington Market. His stepfather had a butter and egg business and we sold the eggs, butter, and cheese. Though we were not very old, the market was so wild that as long as you put money on the bar, they would serve you a beer. We did that every once in a while, just for kicks.

Another time, the market had a party at Coney Island, an amusement park. At that time, it had one of the largest swimming pools. We loved to dive off the tower; it was there that I first got interested in diving. At this particular party, Harry and I won the egg throwing contest, and we should have! We had practiced egg throwing for about a month in advance.

We got up to our fair share of mischief, too. We would ride up the hill on our way home from church by hopping streetcars rather than having to walk. Unfortunately, we pulled the trolley wire off and the whole streetcar had to stop. Someone recognized us, and told Harry's mother. Harry's mother gave us a beating.

Along with my job at Covington Market, I also worked for two weeks on the Island Queen, a riverboat that went from Cincinnati to Coney Island. They had gambling machines on the boat, and I was a money-changer, until they found I had lied out about my age and had to let me go.

I lied about my age rather frequently to find work; another time, I was an usher at the Albee and Grand Theaters. It was a neat job! I wore a uniform, and dated a girl who was a ticket agent in the box office. She was a Japanese and came from Erlanger, Kentucky. She was warm and sweet, despite the fact that her parents were in a relocation camp in California. What was worse, she had two brothers who were interpreters in the U.S. Army. Still, that was how life was at that time.

## YMCA CAMP AND GHOST STORIES

One of the most dramatic changes in my life happened when my grandmother asked if I wanted to go to a summer YMCA camp for two weeks. I immediately said yes. The camp was called Camp Mitcham, located in Kentucky.

When I got there, the Camp Director was short on staff, so he made me a counselor in charge of ten 8 and 9-year-old boys. For an all-camp activity, I invented a ghost story called Headless Hattie, and the rule was that every camper in the cabin had to participate. So, at different times in the story, I would have all the campers in my cabin scream. The story went as follows:

*Hattie Daniels was a 15-year-old farm girl who lived about a mile from Camp Mitcham on a large sheep farm with her parents. Hattie was a tall, slender girl with red hair and blue eyes.*

*Two years ago, around the same time of year, a fellow named Butch (who was 14) was given a free session at this YMCA camp as a reward for good behavior from the Lancaster Boys' Reform Authority.*

*One evening, Butch went riding with another group of campers. Butch was a smart-alec, and he talked the other campers into leaving the group and riding onto a farm that was restricted and out of bounds.*

*There, Hattie was feeding her flock of sheep; they were prized sheep that she had raised from birth. They had won a number of ribbons at a county fair in Kentucky. Butch was showing off and rode the horse right into that flock of sheep trying to scare them. Hattie stood up and tried to stop him. But Butch ran her down.*

*All three of the boys saw that Hattie was seriously injured. They should have gotten off their horses and went to her aid, but Butch shouted, "Let's get out of here because we're in big trouble!" They rode off, leaving Hattie lying there.*

*When her parents found her, they rushed her to a hospital in Cincinnati. Her head had been crushed. A number of operations later, Hattie lived, but part of her brain was destroyed and she only had one eye. Her balance was seriously affected and she had to learn to walk all over again. She managed, but she would stumble and fall and scream out in pain.*

*After a thorough investigation, the Sheriff Department were sure that somebody had run Hattie down with a horse, but they were unable to find out who did it.*

*The next summer, Butch and his two buddies returned to Camp Mitcham, and after a few days, went night riding with the camp group. Again, Butch and his buddy disobeyed the riding instructor and ended up on the Daniels farm once more. When Butch and his buddy were riding into a group of sheep, a figure came out of the night stumbling and screaming. This scared Butch's horse, which ran into a barbed wire fence. When Butch's buddy finally made it back to camp, he told everyone it looked like the figure was carrying a pitchfork, had hair around its neck and one eye in the middle, but no head. Everyone at the camp thought the story was hysterical, and no one believed him.*

*When the county sheriff investigated the crime scene the next day, they found Butch tangled up in barbed wire and they classified his death as an accident. Hattie Daniels was never questioned. But, after that, every time there was a full moon, people have seen this figure stumbling and screaming.*

Now, I thought my cabin would win an award for having the best original all-camp activity. Instead, the Camp Director informed me that there would be no more ghost stories! He had to stop the night riding, too, because 24 campers wanted to go home and he had to convince them it was just a story. He also told me there were a number of bed-wetter's due to the fact that the boys were too afraid to leave the cabin to use the bathroom!

My time at Camp Mitcham gave me perspective and drive to acquire a profession: I knew I wanted to be a Y worker. I soon learned that in order to do that, I would have to have a college degree. This prompted me to stay in school. I stayed with the Y and, even today, am involved with some of the Y programs.

Fifty years later I was at a YMCA camp and they were telling a ghost story…..it was Headless Hattie.

## BACK TO CLEVELAND

My time in Cincinnati came to a close in early 1945 when my Gram and Gramp, who were both in their 80s at that point, found out I was running around with an older group of people that I had worked with at the theater. Gram realized that I was heading for trouble with this group, and she talked to my stepfather. They decided that I might be better off living with my mother's family in Cleveland, and soon after I was on a bus heading there. They never forgot me, though, and every couple of months I would receive a letter from them. They were beautiful people, and I miss them even now.

My mother had died when I was 14, though I hadn't seen her since I was 12. My step-father, at this time, was in the Army and stationed overseas in Burma.

So when I moved to Cleveland, I ended up living with my grandmother. She was a saint; at that time, she had four older women living with us whom she also took care of. They were in the first stages of Alzheimer's, so it was like living in a nursing home. The house was on W. 25th Street in a seedy neighborhood. I was in 9th grade at this point, enrolled at Lincoln High School.

I was a small guy, but remembering what my stepfather had always taught me that no matter where I went, I would run into bullies, and just fight them and get it over with; 9 times out of 10, this would help end the bullying. One day, a senior student who was a starter on the football team intentionally kicked the books out of my arms. This was something the seniors thought was funny, but I didn't think it was so I punched him in the mouth.

Then he kicked me down a flight of stairs. Not only was I banged up, but I was expelled for fighting even though nothing happened to the senior football star. I hated where I lived, and I hated the school. If I could have, I would have quit school then.

At the beginning of the summer, my uncle Carl, who was the foreman at the Bowman's ice cream plant on the west side of Cleveland, was able to get me a job. Most of my work was very repetitive and, consequently, was pretty boring.

One afternoon, I was standing talking to my uncle in the freezer and I had my hand leaning against the wall. When I went to remove my hand, it was frozen to the wall of the freezer. My uncle told me not to move. "You'll pull the skin off your hand!"

He went and grabbed some warm water in a bucket and poured it over my hand until I could finally remove it. When the boss saw what had happened, he laughed and told me, "That'll teach you not to stand around doing nothing!" Everyone joined him in laughing except for me.

A week later, I was carrying a 5-gallon bucket of chocolate up eight steps to pour the chocolate into a large open vat. Unfortunately, there was some chocolate on the top step, and when I stepped there my feet flew out from under me and I fell right into the vat. It already had 7 feet of warm chocolate in it, and I thought I was going to drown. I didn't eat chocolate for a couple years after that.

Though I thought about quitting school and just keeping this job at the factory before the summer started, after doing the same job day in and day out, I decided I would go back to school after all.

I quit the job and spent the remainder of the summer, which was only about two weeks, with my aunt and uncle who lived in East Cleveland. Over there, it was a different world. The people were much more friendly than where I was living on the west side, and the city had a great recreation program. I thought it would be a beautiful place to live.

During my visit, I found out that the East Cleveland YMCA was looking for counselors for a ten-day resident camp called Centerville Mills, and I was able to get the job. It didn't pay, but the food was great and the camp life was enjoyable. While I was there, the program director named Bill Markell offered me a part-time job in the Fall.

I accepted, and I gave him my aunt and uncle's address in East Cleveland. I also got a copy of my transcript from Lincoln High School and enrolled in the 9th grade once more at Kirk Junior High in East Cleveland, using their address again.

That fall, I assisted Bill Markell with some outings and worked in the office at night answering the phones and taking messages. I also supervised the game room. I even did some cleaning and cutting grass.

Even though I had given my aunt and uncle's address, I still lived on the west side of Cleveland. I would get home at 11:30 at night, and I would wake up at 5:00 in the morning to make sure I got to school on time. I loved the school and my job at the Y, but it was killing me.

Mr. Cumler was the director of the Y. When he found out what I was doing each night and morning, he told me, "You can't keep doing this." I thought he was going to fire me, so I told him how I hated living on the west side and how much I loved it at the Y. The next day, he showed me to a clubroom on the third floor of the Y. The building was an old mansion that had been donated to the Y to become the first YMCA in East Cleveland, so there were many rooms.

I was shocked when he said, "I'll let you live here until you find something better. You can use the kitchen and the shower room in the basement. You'll pay your rent by being the night watchman, and maybe this will stop kids from breaking in and stealing equipment and trashing the place."

My aunt Dorothy gave me a single bed and mattress, and a small table and chair. My other aunt, Marion (who also lived in East Cleveland), gave me a little rocker, a pillow, sheets, and blankets. She even gave me a curtain for my window. I was all set with my new home.

One evening at about 11:00 p.m., I heard a sound downstairs, so I went down to the second floor and looked over the rail to the first floor. I noticed a figure going through the coats that were hanging on the wall underneath the rail. I leapt over the rail and landed on the person I thought had broken into the Y. I punched him a number of times, and when he stopped moving I turned on the light. It was Mr. Cumler!

I was so depressed and shook up knowing that I hurt the man who had been so good to me. I thought for sure that I had lost my job and my home, and that I would probably end up back on the west side.

When he came to, however, he didn't fire me. "You were doing your job just as I instructed you to do. Next time I come in after closing hours, I'll yell out so you know it's me." He explained that he had only come back because he forgot his keys in his jacket in the hall closet. I lived at the Y from then, when I was almost 15, until I turned 21.

Mr. Cumler and Bill Markell (who was the assistant director at the Y), were always very helpful. They kept me working and encouraged me to stay in school and plan on going to college, and then maybe I could even become a YMCA director.

YMCA House

# A TRIP TO MARDI GRAS

Just after the first of the year in 1947, my junior year, I stopped to visit two boyhood friends that I had known since the fifth grade at Sackett Elementary School: Jimmy Martin and Tony Graziano (of no relation to Rocky Graziano, the famous boxing champion).

Both boys lived on W. 32nd street just around the corner from my grandmother's house.

This particular visit, they talked me into going to the Mardi Gras in New Orleans, Louisiana. Jimmy's older brother had been to Mardi Gras three different years. He told us of the great parade, the street parties that go on all day and all night, and people all dressed up in Carnival clothes. He told us about the French Quarter, all the bars, Bourbon Street where there were all kinds of music, especially Jazz, and how the Blues and Dixieland bands were singing and dancing everywhere. The only thing he didn't like was there were a lot of beggars, but he said he just ignored them. He said the whole town was decorated, not just the houses, but all along the streets were colorful lights and balloons. It was a city that went all out for Mardi Gras.

I took off a week from school and my work, and it was agreed that the three of us would hitchhike to Louisiana. The reason I think my friends invited me was because I had done a lot of hitchhiking before, and none of them ever had.

I could only raise about $80 for the trip, but the other two had over $300 each so I had to watch how I spent my money. I got maps and planned out a route that

53

we could take to New Orleans. "Whoever gives us a ride," I told them, "we have to make sure we are dropped off in a town or other location where we can get another ride."

Everything was going smoothly until we hit the outskirts of Hattiesburg, Mississippi. There, Jimmy got us a ride with a guy in a little pickup truck, but he dropped us off in the middle of nowhere. I saw a large farm, and I suggested we stop there and find out where we were and maybe we could talk someone into letting us work for a meal.

We went to the farm house, and were told by a hired hand that we would have to talk to Maggie Parsons about work. She seemed like a real nice lady and agreed to give us some work to do, and said we could work off a meal.

The only problem was that they were about to sit down to eat right then. It was only four in the afternoon, so I thought that was strange, but she told us they started work at 5:00 a.m. and they finished at four and went to sleep very early. "I'll tell you what," she said. "you can eat with all of us, and after the meal I will find a job for you."

It was one of the best meals I ever had. We ate like kings, and after the meal she told us to wait on the porch. After she finished with the kitchen help she would come out and put us to work.

As soon as Mrs. Parsons went back into the house my two buddies took off. I told them I couldn't do that. They said, "Suit yourself!" and ran off. When she came back and asked where they went, I told her they took off and I would have to do all the work.

That nice little lady turned into a ferocious monster. "Those good for nothing little bastards! They will wish they had never fucked with Maggie Parsons!"

She then instructed me to stay on the porch. She went inside and called the sheriff. I could hear her. "Sheriff, this is Maggie Parsons." She recounted the whole thing to him, and then said, "I want those two smartass bastards back here, and I have a real good job for them."

About a half hour later, two Sheriff cars pulled up and Jimmy and Tony got out. The Sheriff told Mrs. Parsons that if she wanted they could put them on the chain gang for a couple of months to teach them a lesson.

Thankfully, she said no, but that she would have them clean out one of the duck pens. The Sheriff offered to stick around and see to it that they did their job.

I got up to start to work with my buddies, but Mrs. Parsons told me to just sit down on the porch. She also told me I better start thinking about finding new friends. Later, she brought me a large bowl of strawberry shortcake and ice cream on the porch and told me to wait for my friends to finish their job. "You're judged by your friends," she said. "If you're smart, you'll find new ones."

I never saw the work they had to do, but Jimmy said they had to clean out a duck pen that was about one hundred feet long and twelve feet wide. The floor was covered in shit about four inches deep.

"I'll never eat duck again," Tony said. "In fact, I never want to see a duck again." Tony said that ducks are the dirtiest birds in the world. They eat two ounces of grain, drink two ounces of water, and shit four ounces.

After my buddies finished their work, Mrs. Parsons told us to get off her property and to never come back. The Sheriff told us we would have to walk to the state line, and if they caught us hitchhiking they would put us in the chain gang.

It was just as well we walked. Jimmy and Tony smelled so bad no one would pick us up. Unfortunately, we were about 20 miles from the Mississippi-Louisiana state line.

After a few hours of walking, we came to a little creek. Jimmy and Tony took off their shoes and jumped in to get the smell off, and that night we slept outside in the field. Thank God it was warm.

When we got in New Orleans, Jimmy's brother was right. It was a jumping town, full of all sorts of action.

The first night, we stayed in a YMCA. After that, I didn't see much of my buddies because they planned on robbing "gays and drunks". I thought they would eventually end up in jail. I did see them finally, two days later, and Tony had been beat up so bad he couldn't see. Jimmy thought he had a broken jaw. They had kept to their plan and went out rolling gays. I guess they picked on the wrong guy, because he beat the shit out of them. Then he called the police and had them arrested. They had indeed spent the night in jail, but the police let them out the next morning. In those days, the attitude toward gays was different. They were called "queers" then, and I guess rolling them wasn't considered too serious.

While the guys were out rolling gays, I met a girl named Yolanda. I didn't know she was black until I met her mother, who was very black. Yolanda lived with her mother near the French Quarter. They were very nice people and let me sleep on their front porch. They both worked as cleaning ladies in a downtown hotel. I thought Yolanda was the most beautiful woman I had ever seen. She looked just like a movie star named Hedy Lamarr.

I enjoyed being with Yolanda so much I even went to choir practice with her, and she could really sing! I thought that someday Yolanda might end up in the movies.

Her mother was a good friend of a man named Johnny Smith, who turned out to be the Zulu king of Mardi Gras. He was a big black man who was respected by everyone. He told Yolanda and me where to go to see and hear great entertainment, and was even able to get us into places that we would never have gotten into otherwise.

I really developed an appreciation for Dixieland Jazz and Blues that trip. Two people I heard perform were Al Hirt and Louis "Satchmo" Armstrong.

Yolanda's mother talked Johnny Smith into giving me a job at a restaurant he managed down on the waterfront. I washed dishes from 11 am to 3 pm, I think I made about 30 cents an hour plus a free meal. After three days I got to know Johnny Smith and I thought he was a decent person! He told me that I should not be living at Seath's house because there is a side of her that you don't know, and you don't want to know. He said to be careful because "Yolanda is the bait, and you are the catch".

Yolanda's mother worked at the hotel from 4 pm to 12:00 am, and Yolanda worked from 12:00 am till 8:00am. The first night I slept on the porch, Seath woke me up and told me to come inside. Seath was about 36 years old with a beautiful face and figure (but I thought it strange that she did not shave her legs or armpits). She proceeded to warn me "Yolanda was her baby and that she did not want her knocked up by some white honky, she will never see her again." She told me if I ever touch Yolanda she would castrate me. And from the look on her face, I believed she would. Seath also said that "if you need a woman, I am it," and she took her robe off and stood in front of me stark naked.

Yolanda told me some things about her mother that made me think she was a very strange person. Yolanda told me that she went to a séance where her mother was in charge. Yolanda sat in a circle holding hands with the people on both sides of her, and Seath, her mother, and a young man were in the middle of the circle. The young man was sitting on the ground and Seath stood next to him, speaking in Creole. Yolanda said it was a healing ritual. Each person in the circle said a prayer for the young man, while holding his or her hands at the level of shoulder height. Yolanda said she couldn't hold her hands or arms up any longer, so she let her arms hang down. To her surprise, the people on each side of her, who were very old, held her arms up for her.

One day, I met Yolanda at her house and a man and woman came over with their son who was probably 10 years old. They looked frightened, and they asked to talk to Yolanda's mother. When Seath came out, the boy started to cry. The woman said, "Our son was throwing rocks at your cats and you scolded him and sent him home. We are very sorry that happened and our boy will never do that again." Seath told them they could throw rocks at rats because they're the devil's pets.

Yolanda told me of another mysterious thing that happened. An older woman who worked with Yolanda and Seath brought her daughter in. The daughter looked like she'd been hit by a truck. The older woman explained that the girl's husband, who wouldn't work, would take the girl's pay and squander the money. This time, the girl refused to give her husband the money, because there was no food in the house. The husband was so infuriated he beat her until she couldn't stand up, and then took the money. He had done this a number of times.

She asked Seath if she could help get rid of the husband. Seath told the girl to bring her something that the husband cherished. At the next séance, Seath had a big fire going, and the people sat around the fire. Seath took a Yankees baseball cap that belonged to the young girl's husband, made some remarks in Creole, and threw it into the fire. She told the mother and daughter they would no longer have a problem with the husband.

A few days later, the husband was fishing with three friends in the Okefenokee swamps, and fell out of the boat and drowned. I thought about what Seath had told the mother and figured she was some kind of voodoo witch.

Still, Yolanda was so much fun to be with. She was like a tour guide of New Orleans because she new so much about the history. We would take a streetcar all the way to the end of the line and then walk back home, and the whole time she would tell me stories about this unusual city. She had a fantastic personality and I enjoyed being with her, but at times I felt very uncomfortable around Seath, who would get a very strange look in her eyes.

The only other time I had seen that look was when I was 12-years-old living in Alexandria, Virginia during the World of Mirth Carnival. I had horrible nightmares of the cobra lady staring at me with hate in her eyes. Here was the look again.

I had spent six days with Yolanda, and I enjoyed every minute with her. One day, I was looking for my pocket watch that my step father had given me five years prior. I told Yolanda about my missing watch. Later, she came back and gave me the watch and said she had found it in her mother's drawer. That scared me, because I kept thinking about Seath throwing that man's baseball cap into a fire, and his subsequent death.

The next morning, when Seath and Yolanda went to work, I took all my belongings and left New Orleans without saying goodbye. I took a Greyhound bus from New Orleans to Memphis, Tennessee, and another from Memphis to Cincinnati, and finally one more from Cincinnati back to Cleveland. I know most people think I was crazy for leaving Yolanda, but the mother's hateful eyes disturbed me, and it was time for me to go back to school and work. My week vacation was up. I keep thinking I'll go back to MardiGras someday, though, because it was a real great place to visit.

## LAST YEAR OF HIGH SCHOOL

In my senior year of high school, I had to drop out of school for the year because Mr. Cumler had a connection with one of the officers in the Columbia Transportation Company, and he was able to get me a job as a deckhand on one of their ships working on the Great Lakes. I started working mid-March and had planned to stop in the fall and go back to school, but the steamship company was giving a bonus to all of its employees that worked until the end of the season, which was in the middle of December. I jumped at the offer of a bonus.

Working on the ship, I had plenty of food so I had gone from 164 pounds to 195, and I was in excellent shape. I had planned to play football in the fall, but the head coach informed me that I was ineligible because I had dropped out of school for a year.

In January 1950, I started back at school. I had enough money to be able to buy some nice clothes, a lot of groceries, and enough money left over to go out on dates. Bill Markell gave me a job running the pool as a guard on Monday, Wednesday, and Saturday mornings.

The only problem I had at the Y were the rats that had somehow gotten into the building. They were in the walls and would come out at night. To keep the rats out of my room, I played a small radio all night and left a nightlight on. I didn't complain, because I thought Mr. Cumler knew about the rats.

One afternoon, Mr. Cumler called me into his office and said, "We have a serious problem. This man here told me you are having an affair with his wife!"

I was ready to smash this guy until he jumped up and said, "You're not Bill Bayles! Bill Bayles is about 5'9", weighs about 160 pounds, a little stick but good-looking with thick glasses!"

Right away, though I didn't say anything, I knew he was talking about my friend Jerry Friedlander. Later, when I confronted Jerry, he told me I should be proud that when the girl asked him his name, mine was the first that came to his mind. He wouldn't tell me where she lived. "Somehow, somewhere, I'll get even," I told him.

The opportunity arose about three months later, when Jerry came to me and said he had borrowed his brother's car without his permission, and blew the transmission. He asked if he could stay with me for a couple of days until his brother cooled off. I told him he could sleep on my floor in my sleeping bag.

That night, I didn't turn on the radio or the nightlight. About an hour after we turned in, Jerry started screaming. I turned on the lights and saw the rats. The rest of the night, Jerry sat in the rocking chair with a pool stick, rocking back and forth and saying I was crazy for living with the rats at the Y. I told him I was getting even with him for using my name with that girl and getting me in trouble with Mr. Cumler.

In March, I was living good, but my luck was about to turn. One evening, Mr. Cumler came to my room to talk to me about something. I'll never know what he wanted to tell me, because when he saw that I had a string going from the ceiling light, across the ceiling, and down the wall through eyelets to my bed, he asked, "Aren't you being a little lazy? Why don't you just get up and turn off the light, then walk across the room and climb into bed?"

I told him that there was a reason. My routine was: I would get into bed, make sure that all the covers were tucked all around me, even my head. I would then pull the string to turn off the light. That way, the rats couldn't get me.

Mr. Cumler looked at me like I was crazy. He left my room without saying another word.

It was obvious that Mr. Cumler didn't believe me and I realized that maybe he didn't even know about the rats. So the following Wednesday, which was the day the Y had their monthly dinner meeting, I showed him.

At the end of the meeting, they would put the leftovers in the refrigerator for me, which I greatly appreciated, but they would leave the dirty dishes until they came back the next morning to clean up. After the Y closed that night, I asked Mr. Cumler to meet me at the front door of the Y and to please not make any noise. He only lived a block away, so it was not a problem for him to come and meet me. When he arrived, he asked, "What's this all about?"

"Please just follow me into the building," I replied. It was dark and I slowly opened the kitchen door and turned on the lights. There were more than 20 rats crawling around and having a feast off the dirty dishes.

Needless to say, Mr. Cumler was shocked. He told me when I told him about the rats he thought I was just giving him a line of bull, and he asked why I hadn't said something sooner. I told him I thought he knew about the rats and that I never wanted to be a complainer.

He hadn't known, and he thought it was terrible. "I can't let you stay here. You'll spend the night at my house." The next day, he told me that they were going to fumigate the building and I would have to take all my belongings, including my bed and clothing, to my grandmother's house on the West side until it was okay to move back in.

I packed all my belongings, including the money that I still had left over from when I worked on the lakes. I put everything in a large army trunk that my stepfather had given me. I thought the best place to store the trunk was on a shelf going down into my grandmother's basement, that way no one could get into it. I also tucked my mattress on the side of the basement stairs.

The second night I was at my grandmother's house, I smelled smoke. I opened up the basement door and flames came rushing out. I slammed the basement door and pushed a chair up against it, then told my grandmother that we had to get out immediately, and get all the women out, too.

I was able to get three out of the four women out of the house and then I looked for my grandmother. She was on the stairway trying to pull one of the ladies back down to the first floor. The lady had her arms locked around the banister rails and was unmovable.

I told my grandmother to get out of the house, and that I would get the lady out. She was a big woman, and she wouldn't let go of the banister rails, so I grabbed her and gave a great pull. Together we rolled down the stairs. When we landed she still had the rails in her arms. I carried her out of the front door and onto the porch.

Just then, there was a tremendous explosion on the first floor and all the windows blew out. By the time the firemen got there, the flames were so high that all they could do was contain the fire to keep it from spreading to the nearby houses. I went back to the Y without any clothes or money, not even my mattress.

Near the end of the school year, I stopped into the principal's office and talked to the woman who worked there, Mrs. Crane. I asked her if she would just send me my diploma, because I would not be able to attend graduation. The next day, the principal called me into the office and said that if I didn't attend the ceremony, I was not going to receive my diploma.

That evening, I talked to Mr. Cumler and told him what the principal had said. Mr. Cumler told me not to worry. The next day, he went into the high school and told the principal about my living situation at the Y, and the problem we had with the rats, and how I had lost everything except the clothes on my back in a fire.

A few days later, the principal called me into the office and told me to go to Diamond's Men's Store, at Superior and Euclid Avenue in East Cleveland. He told me to ask for Joe Diamond, the owner, and said he would give me clothes so that I could attend my graduation.

He also asked me who signed my report cards, and I told him that I did it myself. He looked startled.

I later went to Diamond's Men's Store and Mr. Diamond would not let me pick out any of the clothes for myself. He insisted on giving the best of everything: a suit, shoes, a tie, a shirt, and even a set of cufflinks and tie clasp. I asked him how I could pay for these things. He said that I should come back after graduation and we'd work something out.

After graduation, I went back to see Mr. Diamond at least a half a dozen times asking him, "How am I going to pay you back? What do I owe you?"

The last time I went to see him, he said, "Listen, kid. Stop bothering me. I enjoyed helping you. Someday you will run into somebody who needs help, and you will help them, and you'll feel good about it."

Almost 50 years to the day later, my friend Dave Kirschenbaum and I went to West Palm Beach, Florida, to stay in his condo for a week. When we got to the door of his condo, he said, "Just a minute, I want you to meet my next-door neighbor."

When he opened the door, I exclaimed, "Joe Diamond!" He and his wife looked startled, and he said, "Yes, but I don't know you."

That's when I told my friend and Mr. and Mrs. Diamond what Joe had done for me 50 years prior. That week, Mrs. Diamond had me tell the story to four different groups of her friends. "Bill is going to tell you a story about my Joey."

I always remembered what Joe Diamond said about helping someone else. When I went to Kent State College, years after he helped me, I met three students that had financial problems. My wife and I let them stay in our house, rent-free, until they graduated.

# BOOK 2
# The Great Lakes

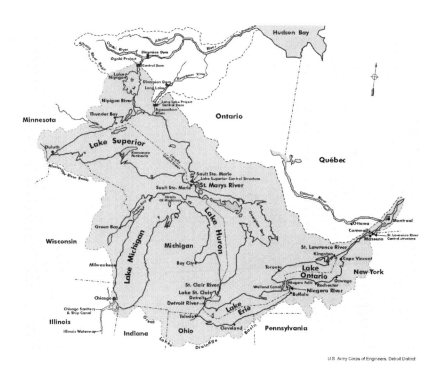

U.S. Army Corps of Engineers, Detroit District

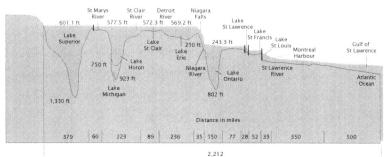

# IVAN ON THE GREAT LAKES

If it weren't for Mr. William V. Cumler, the director of the East Cleveland YMCA, I never would have finished high school. He gave me a job and a place to live at the old Y house, and it was his encouragement that gave me the motivation to complete high school and go on to college.

As stated earlier, In March 1949, in the first half of my senior year in high school, Mr. Cumler helped me get a job working on a steamship on the Great Lakes. Mr. Cumler said "It would be an opportunity to save enough money to get through a year of college, since it pays great and room and board are free". The only problem was I had to drop out of school for a semester as the job started around the end of April. After the work season, I would go back and finish my last year of high school. I was struggling to survive with my limited income, and I decided that with a healthier pay, I could better enjoy my last year of high school.

I ran into a serious problem when I went to get my seaman's papers. I had to submit my birth certificate, and that's when I found out I was not actually adopted even though I used my stepfather's name Bayles, so I brought in my birth certificate which showed my name was William Edward Kilius. I was eventually able to get my Seamens papers, just not under the name of Bayles, but Kilius. I thought that after I completed the season on the Great Lakes, I would have my name legally changed from Kilius to Bayles, which I had used since I was 4 years old.

I was told that I would have a job as a deckhand on a Great Lakes steamship called the William F. Stiefel. This ship was at the Lackawanna docks, in Buffalo, New York. I had to take a train from Cleveland to Buffalo and then a cab to the docks. I arrived on the pier around 11 PM. It was dark and dingy, and there were large rats running around the pier. It gave me an eerie feeling, and I still had to walk about a mile to get to the ship. There was no gangplank to go aboard the ship, just a ladder that went up about 20 feet. I climbed the ladder and when I got on the deck I didn't see anyone, but I could smell a pleasant odor of pipe tobacco.

A few minutes later, a man appeared with a pipe in his mouth and said, "I'm Ivan, the second mate, and I've been waiting for you." Ivan was a small man, at about 5'6", approximately 150 pounds. He looked like he didn't have an ounce of fat on him. He was tan with snow white hair and sharp features. I was surprised a man of his age would still be working on a ship. Ivan showed me the cabin where I'd be sleeping, and then asked me, "Have you had dinner?"

"No sir." He told me to follow him to the galley which turned out to be a large kitchen and dining room. He said, "I'll have coffee, and you can eat. He also mentioned that the galley is open 24 hours a day seven days a week. He didn't realize this, but as soon as he showed me the galley I was sold on working on the ship. It had been many years since I had three square meals on any one given day. Ivan told me since tomorrow was Sunday, I wouldn't have to work, but there would be an orientation meeting. He pointed me to my bed for the night.

When I arrived at my room, there were four bunk beds, and no one was around. One of the lower bunks was covered in old newspapers that had articles and pictures of eight ships that totally disappeared with all crewmembers lost, 248 lives to be exact. There was also a newspaper showing the great storm of 1913, which lasted for six days and was classified as the greatest storm recorded in history of Great Lake navigation. 19 vessels disappeared: ten lost in Lake Huron, three in Lake Michigan, one in Lake Erie, and five in Lake Superior. I figured the crew was aware of my age and that I never worked on a ship before, so they set these newspaper articles out on my bed to rattle me. At the time, I was so dumb that I thought this would never happen to me, because I was a good enough swimmer that I could survive no matter what happened.

A while later, a young man arrived and introduced himself as Danny O'Brien. He and I became the best of friends. Danny saw my bed, and told me, "Don't pay any attention to those articles. Some of the crew think they're funny. They did the same thing to me when I came aboard two weeks ago."

We had a lot in common. It was our first season on the Great Lakes, and we were both from the Cleveland area. Danny was an easy-going guy with a good sense of humor. Unlike myself, Danny was very religious and any time he went to shore he would visit a Catholic Church. Even though I'm not Catholic, I would go with him. I must say I always had a good feeling after being in church. I found out that Danny was also an excellent judge of character, especially when he described members of the crew. He told me that Ivan was the most knowledgeable person on the ship, and the captain wouldn't hesitate telling you that himself.

The next day at the orientation meeting, one of the most important things I learned is you can't let water into the cargo hold, especially if the ships are carrying cargo. If the lake has large waves or a storm we'd have to "batten down the hatches." This means we would put canvases over the hold and clamped them down so that no water could get in. If enough water got into the cargo hold, it could sink the ship.

For my first evening on the ship, Danny took me up to the pilothouse. That's the room where a wheelsman navigates or otherwise steers the ship. This particular evening, Jack Talbot was on duty. Jack Talbot was 60 years old, and had worked on the Great Lakes for 42 years. When the ship was stocked for the winter months, he worked as a security guard or caretaker on the ship and lived aboard all winter. Jack had sailed with Ivan for many years. He loved telling stories about the Great Lakes and especially Ivan. Danny and I loved to hear his stories. He told us that Ivan was a captain on the Great Lakes for over 30 years. "After he had been retired for one year, he couldn't stand it, so he came back to work on a ship as a second mate, which is the position of a troubleshooter." Jack also told us that Ivan is a very quiet man and not very sociable. "But if he tells you to do something, do not question him, just do as he says. You won't regret it and it might save your life." Lastly, Jack also said that Ivan "is a person of high spiritual level." I asked Jack, "What do you mean by that?"

"Ivan is able to acquire knowledge in the same way an animal does. For example, animals can sense that a natural disaster is about to happen, and they'll run from the area and find a safe place." Danny and I both thought Jack Talbot statement about Ivan having a "high spiritual level" to be a little far out, but we certainly didn't tell Jack what we thought.

About two months later, we were on Lake Erie going to Buffalo, New York. It was a Sunday, and that deck crew was off work. Because it was such a beautiful warm and sunny day, we were all out on the deck tanning and getting some sun. Ivan came out of his cabin and told the deck crew, "batten down the hatches!" None of the deck crew questioned Ivan, except the first mate, Mr. Morley, who was directly under the captain, or second-in-command.

"Ivan, that's ridiculous. All the weather reports indicate that it's going to be beautiful for the next three days." Even so, the deck crew did exactly what Ivan told them to do. Sure enough, at about 10 PM that evening, we were in the worst storm that any of the crew had ever experienced. Giant 20 foot waves spilled over the deck. The Captain shouted over the loudspeaker, telling the crew to stay in their cabins and not to go on the deck. If we had not battened down the hatches as Ivan had told us, our ship would've sunk. I thought about what Jack Talbot said, about Ivan having the same instincts as an animal. Later, we overheard the Captain say, "Thank God we have Ivan."

# A HOT SUMMER DAY ON LAKE SUPERIOR

It was a hot summer day and we were at the loading dock in Washburn, Wisconsin. Since it was Sunday, Danny and I had the day off. I talked Danny into going swimming, so we began jumping off the bow of the boat to see how far out we could jump. We had only jumped off the ship twice before we came back aboard and found Ivan was waiting for us. Ivan said, "Captain saw you jump off the bow. He told me, 'Don't those boys know how dangerous it is to jump in this Lake especially around this dock?'" Ivan went on to tell us that we should never jump off of a ship unless the ship is sinking. Jumping in this lake is very dangerous; Lake Superior is the deepest of all the great lakes, the water temperature beneath the surface is almost consistently 39° (just 7° above freezing), although the first 6 feet of the water on a day like this might get up to 50°. If you dive or jump in and go deeper than the surface water you would be in water that is so cold you could go into shock or cramp up.

Ivan then asked us, "Do you know why the captain uses a tugboat to bring our ship into this dock?" We both shook our heads as if to say no. "Several years ago this dock was made of large wooden beams soaked in creosote. When they went to build this new dock, some of the old creosote beams fell into the water and a few of those big beams are still out there floating under the surface. So the reason that the Captain hires a tug boat to bring the ship into the dock is he doesn't want to take the chance that our props might hit one of those sunken logs which could destroy the props or even the shaft that turns it. We could be put out of business. And if you would have hit one of those sunken logs while diving, it could have killed you."

## HENRY SHOOTING SEAGULLS

One morning, I heard gunshots, so I came out onto the deck to find Henry Ledger standing there shooting at seagulls with a 22 rifle. Not long after, Ivan came out on the deck, walked up to Henry and told him, "Killing for food is one thing, but killing for fun is a sin. Seagulls give warning signs to seamen in dense fog. I'll take that gun and I'll give it back to you when you leave the ship."

Later, when Danny and I were visiting Jack Talbot in the pilothouse, I asked Jack, "Why does the crew and the Captain put so much faith in Ivan, and why is he so different than most people?"

"I think it's his heritage, and the way he was brought up."

"What do you know about it?" Danny seemed surprised, "Ivan never told anyone about his background, and what I did hear came from people that knew Ivan when he first came aboard his uncle's ship."

"What I'm telling you is just hearsay, not a positive story," Jack began, "Ivan's parents were Chippewa Indians and lived in Canada near Lake Superior. When Ivan was 10 years old, his tribe was afflicted with a most deadly disease called smallpox. The epidemic killed most of the tribe, including his parents. His grandfather, who survived, was a member of the tribal Council, and was not a chief, but was considered a wise man.

Ivan's grandfather became friends with a missionary and his wife, who had set up a school to teach the English language and Christianity. After the epidemic had subsided the grandfather took Ivan to meet them. He told them that his grandson was 10 years old but, in reality much older than his years would suggest. He said, 'Ivan has a quick mind, if he's told something once he never forgets. He has an inner peace and nothing seems to bother him and he never shows anger. He has the ability to think things through clearly, and has a higher state of consciousness.'

The grandfather then asked the missionary if they would take Ivan. 'My grandson will have no one after I die, and my health is failing.' The missionary and his wife talked it over and decided to adopt Ivan.

From that time on Ivan's last name was Kennedy, and the next two years he lived with the missionary and his wife and they loved him and enjoyed watching him grow. They were amazed by his thirst for knowledge. The missionary had a brother who was a Captain on a Great Lakes steamer and he was able to talk the Captain into taking Ivan aboard the ship to train him for a good job on a steamer. The brother agreed to take Ivan on for the summer, and Ivan worked on that ship from age 14 until age 30.

Because Ivan was so hungry for knowledge and enjoyed the work, the Captain decided to start Ivan at the lowest menial job on the ship which was a porter, an assistant to the cook. When the Captain became aware of how fast Ivan was learning, he promoted him to other jobs until Ivan had worked every position on the ship except as a Captain himself.

Ivan read everything there was to know about the responsibility of running a ship. He would read about the Great Lakes and took every test that was presented to him and of course he passed every course with the highest grade possible. At age 30, the company he worked for gave him a job as Captain on a Great Lakes steamer, and for the next 35 years, Ivan was a Captain with an outstanding record. He retired at 65, but after two years, his wife said 'You're driving me and yourself crazy and you should think about going back to work on the Great Lakes.'

Our Captain not only knew Ivan but was aware of his great track record, so when he heard Ivan was looking for a position on the Great Lakes, he offered Ivan the job as second mate and he has been with us five years. So Ivan is 72 years old. I had worked for Ivan for 10 years as wheelsman on his ship, and when he retired I took a job as the wheelsman and on this ship.

Now you know as much about Ivan as I do, and I think you understand that he is an amazing person."


## BORIS SAZINSKI


One morning, Danny, John Crum and I were out on the deck replacing pipes. They were 4 inches wide and 30 feet long, and it took the three of us to carry just one. As we were hoisting one up, John Crum said, "Look at Boris Sazinski! He's carrying a 30 foot long pipe all by himself," Danny responded, "He's one big guy. He's at least 6'2" and probably weighs 300 pounds and I'll bet his arms are bigger than my thighs. He's amazingly strong."

The next morning, Danny and I were having breakfast at the ship dining room. Boris was sitting at the same table. I don't know exactly why, but Danny started talking about his grandparents that came from Ireland. I made a statement that my grandparents came from Germany and that my grandmother was a saint but my demented grandfather was a Nazi, but before I could say sympathizer, Boris jumped up and threw his chair back.

"I won't sit with any Nazi son of a bitch!" He left the dining room, leaving Danny and me shocked and wondering what that was all about.

Later that evening, Danny and I went up to the pilothouse to visit with Jack Talbot, who was on duty steering the ship. I told Jack about the incident at breakfast with Boris. Jack said, "I'll tell you why Boris acted so strangely. In 1938, when Boris was 16 years old, he and his uncle left Warsaw, Poland and came to the United States. About a year later, Germany invaded Poland and they massacred over 4 million Polish people, most of them civilians. Unfortunately, Boris' entire family was brutally murdered by the German army, so you can understand why Boris feels the way he does." Jack paused a moment. "I'll try and talk to Boris and let him know that you despise your grandfather for being a Nazi sympathizer."

The next day, a bum boat pulled up next to our ship when we were in dock. A bum boat is like a floating store that carries all the things that a sailor could want or need, ranging from medical supplies, to clothes, shoes, and even snacks. When I visited the bumboat, there was a display case that had some unusual knives. I saw one that looked exactly like the one that Ivan carries on his belt. It was very expensive, but I bought the knife because it would always remind me of Ivan. When you pushed a button on the side, the blade came straight out of the handle. A few days later, I saw that my knife was missing out of my locker. I asked Danny if he borrowed my knife, and he said, "No, but I saw Boris carving on a piece of wood and I think it was your knife he was using."

Later at dinner, I asked Boris if he found my knife. He pulled the knife out of his pocket and I could see that it was clearly mine.

"No. This is my knife," and without asking, Izzy and Jim Robertson both said, "Yeah, that's Boris' knife." Izzy continued, "Do you think you are the only one that has a knife like that?" I didn't know what to say. I was so sure that Boris had taken my knife, and Danny thought so to, but we couldn't prove it. I didn't pursue it any further because Boris had his two lying buddies backing him, and I didn't want trouble. Later, John Crum told me that Boris, Izzy, and Jim Robertson are close friends: always together, especially when they go uptown for the evening.

## JOHN CRUM

One evening, Danny and I were up in the pilothouse visiting Jack Talbot, the night wheelsman. Danny asked Jack, "Why is Henry Stewart trying to hurt and embarrass John Crum in front of the other shipmates?"
"Well, what did Henry say?"

"He said to John, 'you must be retarded because no one in their right mind would marry a whore,'
"Henry Stewart should learn to keep his big mouth shut. John Crum is one of the most decent people I've ever met. Let me tell you about John Crum."

"I'll start by telling you the first time I ever met John. It was about 18 years ago, when John was only 18. He came aboard the ship when we were docked in Port Washington, Wisconsin, and the first person he met was Ivan. John said, 'Sir I'm looking for work,' and John handed Ivan a letter written by the head of an orphanage in Milwaukee, Wisconsin. The letter said, 'I would like to introduce you to one of our orphans named John Crum. John has been at this orphanage since age 2, and I think he is an amazing person. He was never a disciplinary problem and was an above average student. He loves to work and if I ever gave him an order, I never had to say it twice. He is well-liked by the staff as well as his fellow students. I am sure that you will never regret hiring John Crum. I think I should also include that John was never adopted because he does not give a good first impression, is very quiet, and sometimes when he gets excited he stutters, and he is not handsome, but if you can overlook these traits you will find a beautiful person.'"

"John has always worked as a deckhand and showed no interest in being promoted to another position, after working on this ship for six years, he met a young woman named Martha Cell. She worked in a house of prostitution, and for two years he saw her every chance he could. After the second year, Martha stopped working as a prostitute and took a job as a waitress. John and Martha spent as much time as possible together, and they fell in love and eventually got married. Between the two of them they had saved enough money to buy a nice home in a city called Manistique located in the upper Peninsula of Michigan, about 100 miles from Sault St. Marie. Whenever our ship comes through the Sioux locks, Martha and their two sons drive up to the locks to visit with John. Sometimes all they can do is wave to each other as the ship moves through the locks."

Danny and I both thought it was a sad situation that some of the crew knew about Martha's past and would make disparaging remarks to John. It was obvious that John was deeply hurt, but never responded to their comments.

On one occasion our ship was laid up for repair at the Sioux locks. Ivan gave John, Danny and I a full day off, and John told us he was renting a car to drive home for the day. He said he had talked to Martha and she invited us to come and visit them at their home and she would cook us an excellent dinner. Danny and I jumped at the chance to get off the ship for a day and told John we would love to go with him.

It was a very scenic ride and when we arrived, Danny and I were both surprised to find the house was large and in a very prestigious neighborhood. The inside was immaculate, and furnished in an early American decor. Danny told Martha she should be an interior decorator. The boys were both handsome, well-dressed with excellent manners. As it turned out Martha was a very beautiful woman, appeared to be well-educated, and for sure was an excellent cook. She was very active in their church, a member of the PTA, and we thoroughly found her to be a gracious lady.

When Danny and I returned to the ship we made sure to tell the crew, especially the ones that were always making sarcastic remarks to John about his wife. After we told them about our trip it was obvious that they should stop making comments to John about his wife.

## RIDING THE LIFELINE

The ship was halfway between Detroit and Buffalo on Lake Erie when a bad storm kicked up. Danny and I knew that we would have to stay off of the deck, because large waves were sweeping over the middle of the ship.

Neither Danny nor I had eaten dinner, so I told Danny the only way we could get to the dining hall was to ride the lifeline. The lifeline was a heavy gauge stainless steel wire with a safety harness hooked onto it. The wire ran from the back of the bow building, which was the building on the front of the ship where the pilothouse is, to the stern building, which was the back of the ship where the engine room, kitchen, and dining area were located.

I told Danny I would go first, and I hooked myself into the harness. I was able to walk the whole length of the lifeline and I took the harness off and sent it back to Danny. He locked himself into the harness and started down toward the dining room. But when Danny got in the middle of the ship, a wave came over the side and swept his feet right out from under him. He went up in the air and landed on his side, but he was able to get back up and make his way to the dining hall. We were both soaking wet from the lake water coming over the side, and I could see that Danny was hurt from when he landed on the deck.

When we got inside the dining hall, the cook came out to meet us with a couple of towels so we could dry off, and he told us there was a message from Ivan giving us an order. It said that we were not to ride the lifeline back to our room, but were to remain in the dining hall for the rest of the night. He would let us know when we could return to our room.

The cook said that the only place we can sleep is on the floor of the dining hall, and then he left to go back to his room. A few minutes later, the porter came with two pillows and two blankets and he said, "I hope you can get a good night's sleep." He went back to his room as well. Danny and I both knew we were in trouble, so we sat down and had a good dinner. In the morning Ivan came into the dining room for his morning coffee. He told us that the Captain saw Danny get hit by a wave and knocked to the deck. "You should know that the lifeline is not entirely safe, and should only be used in an emergency," Ivan said, "I know both of you boys are from the Cleveland area but I bet you didn't know that Lake Erie is the most dangerous of all the Great Lakes. It has had more shipwrecks than all the other lakes combined. It is said that Lake Erie is the shallowest and can act up at any time without giving any warning."

Ivan turned to Danny and said, "I want to see how much damage occurred when you fell on your side." Danny showed him; his right hip and upper leg were black and blue. Ivan said, "We're going to have to keep an eye on you and see if you heal without any complications. I think you've learned a good lesson. The lifeline is not as safe as you thought."

After Ivan left, Danny said, "Now that's two things we have done that has upset the captain.... riding in the lifeline, and diving off the ship."

## A PROBLEM WITH HENRY LEDGER

One Sunday morning, Danny and I heard a commotion out on the deck, so we went out to see what was happening. Izzy was yelling at the first mate and Henry Ledger.

"I bought that expensive scotch to give to my brother for his birthday! It was wrapped as a present, and I had no intention of drinking it!"

When Danny saw Jack Talbot standing on the deck, he asked Jack, "What's this all about?" Jack said, "Izzy bought liquor for his brother's birthday, and it was wrapped and in his locker, and Henry had no business going in there." The first mate told us that there was an unwritten rule stating that no crew-member could bring alcoholic beverages aboard the ship, and so the first mate threw the bottle over the side.

A week later, we were in Toledo, Ohio unloading more than 100,000 tons of iron ore. Once all the holds were empty, four of the crewmembers were down in the hold cleaning out any of the ore that was left on the floor. Up above, two crewmembers were on the deck with ropes tied around 5 gallon buckets. They would drop down these buckets into the hold, and the cleaning crew would put the waste that they had collected into the buckets.

Izzy was one of the crewmembers pulling the buckets of waste up from the hold and throwing the waste over the side of the ship, and Henry Ledger and I were down in the hold filling the buckets of waste. As I looked up out of the hold, I saw Izzy pulling up a bucket of waste that had to weigh at least 60 pounds. I watched Izzy, and I realized he was waiting to get Henry right under his weighted bucket. As soon as he saw that the bucket was right over Henry's head, he let go of the rope holding the bucket. As I saw the bucket come down, I shoved Henry out of the way and as it hit the ground, the bucket actually made a dent in the metal floor.

Ivan was up on the deck and observed what almost happened. It was obvious that Izzy was trying to kill Henry. Later, when the crew had finished cleaning up, we were all standing on the deck and Ivan said to Izzy, "You were trying to drop that bucket on Henry, and if Kilius hadn't pushed Henry out of the way, you probably would've killed him."

"No, the rope just slipped out of my hand."

"You probably have the strongest hands of anyone on the crew so I doubt that the rope slipped away from you... and if you had injured Henry I would've had you arrested, so Kilius not only saved Henry's life but he probably saved yours too."

One evening, after dinner, Ivan called Henry, Boris, Izzy, and Mike and told them to meet him in the wheelhouse in one hour. Jack Talbot was also at the wheelhouse steering the ship.

There, Ivan told Izzy, Boris and Mike to sit and listen. To Henry, Ivan said, "I'm going to ask you some questions, and if you lie to me I'm going to fire you right here on the spot." Then Ivan turned to Jack Talbot and said, "You are a witness." Jack nodded his head as if to say "okay".

"Henry did you tell Izzy, Boris and Mike that I said that I despise them because they were drunks and spend all their money on whores and booze and depriving their families of a decent living? Did you also say I always sat facing the wall when I ate dinner because I couldn't stand the sight of them?" Ivan asked. "Did you tell them that I said these things to you?" And Henry said, "yes, sir."

"Now did I ever say anything to you about any member of this crew? Answer me!" Ivan yelled.

Henry responded, "No sir, you never told me anything about anyone on this ship."
"In other words, you made up the story," Ivan said.
"Yes, sir."
"Henry, I feel that anyone who makes up stories like this is a dangerous troublemaker, and if you ever do anything like that again I'll not only fire you, I'll see that you lose your seamen's card and never work on the Great Lakes again. Since some of you wonder why when I eat dinner I sit facing the wall, it's because I only eat one meal a day, and I don't want to get involved in conversations. I thoroughly want to enjoy my meal. Are there any questions?" The crew said, "No sir."

They got up and left the pilothouse. After Ivan left, Danny and I went up to the pilothouse to talk to Jack Talbot. We asked him, "What transpired with Ivan and the four crew members?"

Jack Talbot said, "I'll tell you what happened if you promise to never repeat what I'm telling you, and if you do I'll never talk to you again" We both promised. Jack Talbot told us all about the meeting, and then he said, "I was the one who told Ivan about the lies Henry told the three crewmen… there are things that you should know about Henry Ledger. First of all, Henry's father is a captain on the Great Lakes and friends with our captain, so it is obvious that Henry has some good connections. Henry is very knowledgeable and book smart, but he has no common sense. He offends people and says things he shouldn't and is a liar, and doesn't care how he hurts people. Three years ago, John Crum made a terrible mistake and thought that Henry Ledger was his friend. John told Henry how his wife had changed her life around from a life of sin to become a lady with high moral standards. The reason I'm telling you all this so that you know not to trust Henry Ledger, and have as little to do with him as possible."

A few days later, I was going uptown to the movies to see a picture called We Were Strangers with Jennifer Jones, John Garfield, Gilbert Roland, and Pedro Armeneaz. As I was walking up to town, Henry Ledger caught up with me and asked me where I was going. I told him I was headed to the movies and he said that's where he was going, too. At that point, I thought about turning around and going back to the ship but I really wanted to see that movie, so I went with him.

When we got to the theater, we were one hour early, so Henry said we could go in this bar nearby and kill an hour by drinking a couple beers. I agreed, and when we entered the bar, I noticed six of our crew members were in the bar drinking. Two of the men I knew, Kermit Housman and Jim Portman (nicknamed "Horse" because his front teeth were as large as a horse's teeth). Danny and I used to enjoy watching Kermit hit a small punching-bag. Kermit worked in the engine room as an oiler; he was forty years old, about 5'8", weighed 165 pounds, and was in excellent condition. We were told that Kermit was a Golden Gloves champion in Detroit, Michigan, and had a number of professional fights.

Kermit's friend Horse was a coal-passer and was 22 years old. Whenever you saw Kermit, Horse was always with him and we thought that Horse probably idolized Kermit. Henry and I went over to where Kermit was seated, and Kermit was showing some crewmembers the expensive perfume that he bought for his wife. When Kermit saw Henry he sprayed Henry in the face and told him to get lost.

Henry immediately turned around and left the bar, but I stayed and ordered a Coke. When the Coke came, Kermit grabbed the Coke and dumped it in the sink behind the bar and told me to get lost, too. I said, "I'm not with Henry and I'm not leaving." Kermit spun me around on the bar chair and slapped me across the face, when I went to punch him he blocked my punch and hit me about 15 times, giving me a fat lip and a black eye. I picked Kermit up and was going to throw him into the ground when the bartender stepped in and told me I had to leave. Kermit said to me, "Don't come to any bar where I am or I'll kick your ass." I said, "You don't tell me where I can or can't go. I'll see you later."

I didn't go to the movies, instead I just returned to the ship. When Ivan saw me with a black eye and a fat lip, he didn't say anything, he just shook his head and walked away.

A month or so later, our ship was back in Ashland, Wisconsin. I walked into the same bar where Kermit had started a fight with me and sure enough Kermit and his friend Horse were there. I sat at the end of the bar away from Kermit. He said, "I told you not to come around where I am at."

I immediately turned around on the barstool and stood up facing Kermit waiting for him to start swinging. What I didn't notice was that Horse had kneeled down behind me. When Kermit stepped forward I tried to step back and fell over Horse and hit my head on the bar rail. I cut my head and was bleeding real bad. The owner of the bar saw what happened and told Horse and Kermit to get out before he called the police. Then the owner gave me a towel with ice wrapped in it and he told me that I better get that cut looked after.

As I walked down the street, I passed a restaurant and I heard someone knocking on the window. It was Ivan, motioning for me to wait for him outside. He was just about to sit down and eat, so I assume he told the proprietor he couldn't stay. Ivan came outside and took the towel off of my head and said, "That's a nasty cut, I'm taking you to the emergency room."

After the doctor sutured my head and gave me an antibiotic to put on the cut, Ivan told me I had lost too much blood and he was calling a cab to take me back to the ship. While driving back, Ivan wanted to know how I got the cut, and when I told him what happened he said, "From now on, stay out of the bars. That way you won't get into any trouble." I said, "Yes sir."

Our next trip was to Port Washington, Wisconsin. We were delivering a load of coal briquettes. Danny told me that Kermit was leaving the ship to go home and take care of his wife, who was very ill. Ivan was hosing down the deck with a high-pressure hose, and I was on the shore waiting to move the cables that hold the ship in one place. When I saw Kermit carrying a large duffel bag, I ran over and stood in front of him and said, "We're not through yet."

He threw the bag down and came at me. We started punching and rolling around in the coal. When I was on top of Kermit, Horse came running over carrying a large school shovel and was going to hit me. But Ivan was watching and hit Horse with the hose, the pressure of the hose sent Horse flying back. Ivan said, "Either go with Kermit, or get back aboard the ship now." Then Ivan hit both Kermit and I with the hose, as well. Ivan ordered me to get back on the ship and he said to Kermit, "You had that coming, now go home and take care of your wife."

I ended up with some loose teeth and another black eye. Afterward, Ivan said to me, "Well do you feel better now?" I said yes, but he only laughed and walked away.

## AN EVENING OUT WITH DONNIE HUDSON

Donnie Hudson was the night wheelsman, and he worked from midnight to 8 in the morning. He taught Danny, John Crum and me how to play pinochle, which was an excellent card game that filled a lot of our spare time. Donnie told us he had only worked on this ship for three years, but worked on another ship on the same line for five more. He joined the Navy in 1942, and just after he graduated from high school, he became a Navy fighter pilot during the second world war. Donnie said the reason he walks with a limp is because his plane crashed and he injured his leg. He retired at 20 years old with a medical disability and then enrolled at Kent State University on the G.I. Bill. After four years, he received a bachelor of science degree in education. He taught junior high school for one year and hated it, and that's when he took a job on the Great Lakes. After five years, he became a wheelsman. Donnie never married, and lived with his mother in Willoughby Ohio. He had his pilot license and owned a small Piper Cub plane, which he kept at the Willoughby Ohio airfield, and flew whenever he had the time.

One evening, Donnie Hudson asked Danny and me if we wanted to go see a movie called She Wore a Yellow Ribbon. It was supposed to be an excellent Western featuring John Wayne. We were docked in Duluth, Minnesota but the movie theater was across the bay in Superior, Wisconsin. Donnie said he would pay for the cab but we would have to pay for our own movie and dinner.

After we saw a great movie and had dinner, Donnie looked at us and said, "I want to show you an unusual place, called the St. Paul Rooms." Of course, when we arrived it turned out to be a cat house.

Danny was aghast. "I'm not interested. I'm engaged to be married, and if my girlfriend ever found out, I think she would call off the wedding."

"This is the kind of a place you could contract a venereal disease." I wasn't interested either.

"Come on, let's just see what the place looks like and have a beer and we won't stay long." When we went inside, I was surprised, because the place was very well furnished with a beautiful bar and quite a few men standing around drinking and talking. The three of us ordered a beer from a young waitress, and Donnie said he had to use the restroom. Before he came back, a pretty woman came up to me barely wearing a thin bathrobe. I was embarrassed because everybody was looking at us.

"Are you interested?" she started to say, but before she could finish saying "interested," I noticed she had a large open infection on her side and I shoved her away. She flew across the floor and started to cry. Donnie saw everything as he returned from the bathroom.

"Let's get out of here." We had just made it out the door when three men came and grabbed me. Two grabbed an arm while the third guy started punching me in the stomach. Danny, reacting, punched the guy that was hitting me and knocked him out cold. All of a sudden we were surrounded by four policemen with billy-clubs who broke up the fight. It was obvious that the police knew the three guys from the cat house.

They told Danny and I that we were under arrest and would be charged with disorderly conduct. Donnie stepped in and said this is all a terrible mistake and told them what went on inside, but the police did not appear to be interested. Eventually, they relented.

"We'll take you back to your ship. You're lucky we're not putting you in jail." Donnie asked if he could go with us. When we came aboard, Ivan looked shocked.

"What's going on here? Why did the police bring you back to the ship?" Donnie again stepped in.

"It was all my fault, I should never have taken them to the St. Paul Rooms." Donnie elaborated, "As a joke, I gave one of the girls $10 to go sit on Bill's lap. But he didn't realize the girl had psoriasis on her hip. I have it too, so I wasn't worried about it. I keep it under control with medication and sunlamp treatments. But I'm sure Bill thought she had some terrible venereal disease and he shoved her away. The staff thought Bill intentionally hurt the girl, so they went after him and Danny. I made a terrible mistake, and I'm sorry."

Ivan stood up and just shook his head and walked away. We didn't end up getting into trouble but Donnie sure took a ribbing from the crew.

## IVAN BEING INJURED

On one cold and rainy night, we had just picked up a load of sand in Saginaw, Michigan. Ivan was standing on the deck watching the ship pull away from the dock, when all of a sudden a strong gust of wind swept his legs right out from under him. I thought he was going over the side and into the lake. He landed hard on his back, then slid forward and his leg caught on a post that holds the deck rail up. I knew he was hurt bad because he just laid there. Thank God for the ship's rail, because that's the only thing that stopped Ivan from going over the side.

I pulled him up off the deck and under an overhang, "Are you alright?" He grunted, "No, help me to my room." After moving him to his chambers, I noticed there was blood on the inside of his right leg seeping through his pants and running all the way down into his shoe. Ivan sat down in a lounge chair and he put the injured leg up on a foot rest. "There is a pair of scissors in the drawer of my bookcase. Bring it here." I did as he instructed. "Good. Now cut the pant leg off at the knee." He kicked off his shoe, and as soon as I cut off the pant leg, I could see a nasty gash on the inside of his lower leg. Ivan had me get a first-aid kit from the lower drawer of his bookcase, and told me how to take care of the wound. Then he had me take the pillowcase off the bed, go to the dining room and put ice in the pillowcase. When I came back to the room, he told me to put the ice pack on the chair behind his lower back. It appeared that he hurt his back more than his leg. "I want you to stay here in the room tonight in case I need something and you are not to tell anyone what happened tonight."

"Yes, sir." Every half hour he instructed me take the ice pack off and put it back on in a half hour. After a couple of hours, he had me take the ice and put it in his bathroom sink. "I'm comfortable in this chair, so I'm going to stay and try and get some sleep." He had me get a bottle of pills off of his dresser, and took two. I figured they were sleeping pills. Finally, he told me to turn on the radio and leave it on the station that it's on because that station only plays music, and within a half hour, he was asleep.

I was surprised to see that Ivan had a stack of the Wall Street Journal. I found out later that Ivan was very wealthy and he made a lot of money on the stock market. I remember John Crum saying that Ivan gave John's wife some stock market tips which she invested in.

The only picture Ivan had in his room was a picture of his wife standing between two large German Shepherd dogs. John Crum had also mentioned that he wrote a letter to his wife each week when he was aboard the ship. Whenever they were in the Detroit River, in the daylight hours Ivan could be seen standing on the deck looking over on the Canadian side in Windsor, Canada, and his wife would be standing on the pier with their two dogs. Ivan and his wife would wave to each other. At 6 in the morning, Ivan had me go to the kitchen and bring back a pot of coffee. "Remember, you're not to tell a soul what happened last night."

## AN UNENJOYABLE TRIP
## TO PORT HURON, OHIO

On Saturday, August 1st, we pulled into Port Huron, Ohio to drop off a ship load of grain. There were two ships ahead of us, so Ivan gave the deck hands the day off. Danny O'Brien's girlfriend and her parents came to pick up Danny and take him into Bay Village, a suburb of Cleveland. When I found this out, I asked Danny if I could bum a ride into Cleveland. He checked with his girlfriend's parents and they said they would be happy to give me a ride into Cleveland.

When I got there, I took a bus to East Cleveland, a suburb where I had been living for the past four years. There were three things I planned to do before returning

94

to the ship. The first was to visit the old Y House where I lived.

When there, I called one of our football coaches, George Hucksel, who was also a good friend. "Mr. Hucksel, I'm hoping to get a football scholarship. When will practice begin? I gained 30 pounds. I went from 160 to 190 and I'm in excellent shape."

"Bill, I'm sorry to tell you this but because you were not in school the previous semester, you're ineligible." He was sorry but there was nothing that could be done.

At the old YMCA House, I visited with Mr. Cumler, the man who helped me get the Great Lakes job. I told him how much I like my job, the places I visited, and especially that I was getting three square meals a day. I thanked him and I told him that I wasn't going to be able to play football, so I think I'll stay aboard ship until the end of the shipping season. If I stayed, I'd get a $500 bonus.

The last and most important thing I was going to do was visit my girlfriend. I went to her house, but was told by her cousin that she was out with an ex-boyfriend of hers. I was hurt, and thought this is not been a very good day for me. I hitchhiked back to the ship.

We didn't get to unload until Monday morning because the ground crew didn't work Sundays. To unload the ship, the ground crew used a grain elevator which is a long belt with scoops on it that carries grain from the lower level up to a silo, a 40-foot high tank. Our job was to open the hatches that protect the grain, so a ground crew could access the hold to unload.

We'd just finished opening the hatches, when the wind sent Boris's baseball cap flying off his head, into the hold and on top of the grain. I was used to jumping into the hold when we were carrying coal, sand and ore, but this was the first time we'd carried grain. I guess I thought it was no different. I jumped after the hat into the grain and sunk into it like water. No matter how I moved, I was sinking deeper and deeper. I thought I was going to smother to death.

Up on the deck, Ivan quickly grabbed a heaving line, wrapped it around Danny's waist, and told him to jump after me-- "If you grab him, or if you want to come out, pull twice on the heaving line!" When Danny jumped in, his foot bumped into me, and I grabbed ahold of his leg. He reached down and grabbed my shirt and, then pulled twice on the line. Boris pulled us out of the grain, then out of hold, and then up to the deck. After I washed the grain out of my eyes, I could see the captain was standing there on the verge of a nervous breakdown. Ivan noted, "I guess you learned a lesson: you never jump into grain because you'll be smothered to death."

"That's the most helpless feeling I've ever had in my life." Later, I told Danny about my trip into Cleveland, and that I was sorry I ever came to Huron, Ohio.

## SAVING IZZIE'S LIFE

One evening, I had gone out late to see a movie, and I was walking along the pier when I noticed a figure ahead of me. He was staggering. When I got closer I realized it was Izzy. "Izzy you're getting too close to the edge of the pier!"

I guess he didn't hear me, because he fell into the water between the pier and our ship. I ran over, dove in and grabbed him. I had to wedge myself so that my feet were touching the side of the pier and my back was against the ship. Izzie was very thin but with the wet clothing and shoes he was heavy. I knew I had to move fast because if another ship came down the river and passed us, their waves would push our ship closer to the pier and crush us.

So I had him laying over my legs, his head down on one side and his legs on the other. With my hands, I pushed us up on the side of the ship, and with my legs, I walked up the side of the peer. When I got high enough, I rolled Izzie off of me and onto the shore. I knew Izzie was alive because he was mumbling something. I was exhausted.

I must have laid on the pier for ten minutes before I could even stand up. I dreaded carrying Izzie up the ladder, but I couldn't leave him laying on the pier, so I threw him over my shoulder with his legs in front and his head behind me.

I got halfway up the ladder before the ladder started to sway in and out. I moved very slowly until I reached the deck. What was strange was I could smell Ivan's pipe, but he was nowhere to be seen.

I took Izzy to his room and laid him on his bunk. I guess when I was carrying him up the ladder, he must have threw up, because I had vomit all over the back of my legs. I left Izzy on the bunk fully dressed, with his shoes on, and I went to take a shower and wash and dry my clothes.

The next day, Jack Talbot told Danny and me that Ivan saw everything that happened last night, from the time Izzy fell in the water until I put him in his bunk. Jack said Ivan told him about the incident.

I saw Izzie, Boris and Jim Robertson at the dining hall and I heard Izzie saying someone threw a bucket of water on him and his bunk and he said, "I bet it was Danny O'Brien or Bill Kilius." At that point, I couldn't help myself. I had to tell Izzie what really happened. "Last night I saved your life, and if you don't believe me, ask Ivan, because he saw everything," I said. Jack said to Izzy, "What a jerk you are, Kilius saved your life." None of the three men said anything, so I walked away.

## AT THE TOLEDO DOCKS

One evening, while on Lake Erie pulling into the docks in Toledo, Ohio, we found ourselves in a terrible rainstorm with high rolling waves. The ship was sitting high in the water since our holds were empty.

Ivan told me he would have to put me out on the shore using our landing boom, a 16-foot long pole that sat on an 8-foot high post. The boom had pulleys at each end with a long, heavy gauge rope that ran through the pulleys. Ivan would stand on the deck with the rope at the one end, and at the other end of the boom there was a chair that looked like a swing. I sat down in the chair and Boris swung the boom away from the ship as Ivan lowered me down onto the peer. Once I was on solid ground, Boris threw me a heaving line with a handle that was attached by cable to the ship, which I attached to a post anchored into the peer, a "spile." Once secure, the cable was wound up by a machine aboard the ship called a wench. By winding up the cable, it brought the ship closer to shore and even stopped the ship and held it in place.

I was on the shore holding the end of the cable as the ship was moving down the pier and heading back out into the lake. The process involves manually switching the onshore cable from spile to spile. The ship was moving so fast and the wind and rain was flying into my face, that I missed one--but I thought there was another further down the pier. What I didn't realize was that I had passed the last spile on the pier and I was extremely close to flying off the dock and into the river. Once in the water, the ship would've probably crushed me.

From the deck, Ivan, Boris and Danny were yelling at me to drop the cable, but the storm was so noisy that I couldn't hear them. Fortunately, John Crum handed Ivan a portable loudspeaker. That's when I first heard Ivan say "drop the cable!" I dropped it, and finally noticed I was only 2 feet away from falling off the end of the pier. The captain saw everything. This was another time I traumatized him and Ivan.

The next morning, the storm had passed over and it was a nice clear day. We were waiting for our turn to have the ship loaded with sand. John Crum told Ivan, "hey, there is a raccoon down in the hold and Henry Ledger said if you would give him his 22 back he would shoot it," Ivan replied, "Absolutely not. No one's going to shoot that raccoon." He told the staff that raccoons are beautiful animals but they can be very dangerous, and they have been known to attack people. If you are attacked by a raccoon you need to go to the hospital immediately since they could have rabies. I remember I'd read a survey claiming about a third of the raccoons in this country carry rabies.

That same morning, Ivan went into Toledo and bought a small cage, figuring we could catch the raccoon. Three times we put food in the cage, but three times the raccoon picked the whole thing up and dumped out the food and ate it. When we told Ivan what the raccoon did, he only laughed. "They are smart animals. Let's try bolting the cage down so he can't turn it over and maybe will catch him."

Sure enough, it worked, and soon we had a caged raccoon. I told Ivan, "I'll take the cage down to the shore and let the raccoon out," but Ivan said he wanted to take care of it himself. We later found out Ivan rented a cab and took the raccoon out to the country to let it go. Some of the crew thought Ivan was really strange for going through all that trouble just to get rid of the raccoon, but the people who knew Ivan's heritage understood that most Indian tribes consider those animals to be sacred.

In the early afternoon, a tragic thing happened. The area around the pier was always so loud with machines running, but all of a sudden there was complete silence. John saw that people were flocking to the ship behind us, so we went over to look. There must've been 100 people standing there, looking down in the ship's hold. We were told that the pier's overhead crane bucket had come down and crushed one of the crewmembers. I didn't want to see the crushed seamen. I thought this trip to Toledo was very unusual. I could've been just as easily been killed if I hadn't heard Ivan yelling to me.

# A PLEASANT SURPRISE

One evening, after dinner, Danny said to me, "Don't you wonder where Boris, Izzie and Jim Robertson go every time they go into town? And they always go together."

"It's almost certain they go to a bar, because when they return to the ship all three of them look like they're half in the bag." We had nothing else to do, so we set out to find them.

Danny and I walked around the town for over an hour and checked out every bar, but with no luck. We were about to go back to the ship when we heard music playing as we passed a small hotel. I said, "let's go inside the hotel and see where the music is coming from." The hotel had a small dining room with a bar, and there was a man playing the piano, another fellow singing and there also was a man who had a coat hanger in each hand with a metal standing ashtray. He was using the ashtray as a drum and was keeping time with the music. Danny said,

"My God, that's Boris singing." I looked over.

"That's not only Boris, that's Izzy playing the piano and Jim Robertson keeping time with the music." We stood outside the dining room for a while and listened. Danny said, "They're really good, let's go inside and listen."

"I don't know. Boris hates me, and I don't want to be thrown out."

"Jack Talbot talked to Boris and told him you despised your grandfather because he was a Nazi sympathizer. Also, Boris is the one that pulled us out of the

grain, and don't forget they know you saved Izzie's life."
So we went inside and sat at a table as close to the piano as
possible. We knew we couldn't just sit there for free, so we
ordered a hamburger, fries and a Coke. We stayed there
and listen to the music for two hours, and we drank six
cokes a piece. Danny asked me, "Remember when Ivan
told Izzie you intentionally dropped that bucket and
could've killed Henry Ledger? Izzie said the rope slipped
out of my hand, Ivan said, 'I doubt that because you
probably have the strongest hands of any of the crew.' I
know why Ivan said that. I heard that piano players' hands
are amazingly strong, because they built up their fingers
playing the piano." I thought about it for a moment.

"And remember when Henry claimed Izzie, Boris
and Jim Robertson are spending their pay on booze and
depriving their family of a decent living? I don't think these
fellas spend a penny on drinks because all the people sitting
and listening to them are buying them drinks." Boris had a
beautiful tenor voice and Izzi was an outstanding piano
player. Jim Robertson could've been a drummer because
he kept real good rhythm with the music. Boris was singing
some songs that Nat King Cole made popular such as
Unforgettable, Mona Lisa, Cold Cold Heart and Two
Young. That night, Danny and I had the most enjoyable
evening that we ever had on the Great Lakes. What a
pleasant surprise, and who would've thought that those
three tough guys were so talented!

# IVAN ON THE DETROIT RIVER

One Sunday evening, Danny and I went up to the wheelhouse to spend some time with Jack Talbert, and we asked Jack what our next destination was.

"We're dropping off coal briquettes at Port Washington, Wisconsin and then on to Ashland, Wisconsin." A few minutes later, the Captain came into the pilothouse and told Jack Talbot that he was waiting for Ivan. When Ivan arrived, the Captain announced that he had just received a weather report: "The Detroit River from the Lake Erie Shores to Lake Huron is in a dense fog. Most of the ships are anchored outside of the river at both ends, and we should probably do the same but we're running late."

Ivan straightened up, "I can take you through the fog. We have a couple things in our favor. First, most of the boats won't dare go on the river when there's such a heavy fog. Second, we will be travelling against the current which makes the ship easier to steer. We have about an hour before we get to the Detroit River so have the first mate get on the radio and see if there are any boats coming down the river from Lake Huron." Danny and I were about to leave the wheelhouse when the Captain told us, "You can stay, but you must be quiet when we get to the river."

I asked Ivan, "How long is the Detroit River?"

"It's 28 miles long and the channel is 50 feet deep and 400 yards wide. So, ships going up the river have 200 yards to maneuver and the ships coming down the river have 200 yards to maneuver, and the trick is always knowing where you're at on the river. I plan to keep the ship as close to the Canadian side of the channel as possible, leaving plenty of room for ships coming in the opposite direction."

"Okay. How fast will we be going?"

"10 knots." I guess Ivan realized we didn't know anything about knots, so Ivan said, "10 knots is 11 ½ mph, so it should take us less than three hours to get out of the river and into Lake Huron. I'll be out on the deck and you must be very quiet." He looked at Jack Talbot, "I'll have both my arms up, and if I point to the right side you start turning the wheel slowly right, and when I bring it back up that means stop. My left arm will be up and if I drop my arm that means steer to the left slowly and again if I bring my left arm back up you stop. If there is a serious problem, I'll turn facing you and tell you to cut the engines. We might have to throw the ship in reverse to stop it." Ivan walked out on the deck and asked Jack, "Can you see me?" "Yes sir", he answered.

Meanwhile, the Captain had a worried look on his face, "I've never seen such dense fog. Thank God that Ivan is so intuitive with his sense of direction. Nobody knows the Detroit River better than Ivan." Danny asked, "What exactly is Ivan listening for?"

"None of us know, but we're not going to question him." When we had been on the river for two hours, it seemed like everything was going smoothly when all of a sudden the Captain cried, "Damn!" We looked over, and a ship was coming in the opposite direction, right next to us. Danny said, "It's so close I could jump on!" The other ship sat about 4 feet lower than we were. The Captain noted,

"That ship has a full cargo, while ours is only carrying a half a load. So we sit higher in the water."

Ivan yelled back to the Captain, "Call that ship immediately and tell him he is on the wrong side of the channel! He's lucky that he didn't hit us."

An hour later, we were out of the river and in Lake Huron. When the Captain and Ivan left the wheelhouse, Jack Talbot said, "Thank god we have Ivan. He's our guardian angel." Danny only said, "What an exciting evening."

*Ivan Kennedy*

# A PLANE RIDE WITH DONNIE HUDSON

One evening, Donnie Hudson came to Danny and me and said, "I still feel bad about taking you to the St. Paul Rooms and getting you into trouble, but I have an idea how I can make it up. Tomorrow's Sunday and we have the day off, I can rent a small plane and take you for a ride and do some sightseeing. If you agree, I'll call a cab in the morning and take us to the airport. Danny and I agreed to go with Donnie. Both of us were looking forward to the next morning.

The next morning, we got in a cab and Donnie took us to a small airfield on the outskirts of Duluth, Minnesota. We walked over to the plane. It looked new and in beautiful shape, Donny said, "this plane is called the Piper Cub, and I have one at home exactly like it. It is one of the safest and best light planes there is, and they sell more of these planes than any other small plane in the world. It can land and take off where no other plane could."

We got in, and Donnie said, "The first thing you must learn is to fasten your seatbelt." This plane only had three seats, one for the pilot and two passengers. He continued, "We're lucky. The weather forecast shows this is a perfect day for flying. Light winds, no clouds, and the temperature is 68°, so we have good visibility. This is the third time I've rented this plane this year so I know where to fly to where there's nice scenery."

When we were up in the air over Lake Superior, I know Danny was a little nervous and so was I. Danny asked Donnie,

"How fast are we going?" "Well, we're going 70 miles an hour, but this plane can get up to 85 mph. This is a good cruising speed." We kept going, flying over the Minnesota ore fields. They reminded me of a strip mine I had seen in Maryland. There were overhead cranes, bulldozers, trucks, and train cars, and they had stripped the land and made it uninteresting.

The Lake superior shoreline was beautiful. Donnie pointed out a small Chippewa Indian village. It looked like a lot of small buildings, I told Donnie,"I thought it would look a lot different!" Donnie started to laugh. "What did you think, the Indians still live in teepees?"

We flew over a number of cargo ships and they looked so small from the air. I asked Donnie if we'd be able to see the Sioux lock and Donnie said,

"The Sioux locks are 500 miles away, so we won't be able to see that today."

We continued on. We saw the largest grain elevators in the world in Superior, Wisconsin. They looked to be about 300 feet tall. We saw the Gooseberry Waterfalls and the River Gorge flowing into Lake Superior. It was a spectacular view. We flew over to the Split Rock Lighthouse, and we also saw two other lighthouses, one called Two Harbors Lighthouse, and the other Duluth North Lite-house and pier. They were all different and beautiful.

On the way back to the airfield, Donnie buzzed our ship. That was the only time I was truly scared. He dropped down so fast, I thought he was going to crash into our ship. I thought Ivan would say something about Donnie buzzing our ship but he never mentioned it. When

Donny landed I was glad to get back on the ground, and we thanked Donnie and said, "You sure made up for taking us to the Saint Paul Rooms."

## AN ACCIDENT ON THE SAULT ST. MARIE

It was November 4th, and we were coming into the Sioux Locks. It only takes about an hour to go through the locks, and ships have to wait their turn to enter. One by one they are dragged forward using cables attached to an onshore spile. Once inside the lock chamber, enough water drains out to lower the ship 21 feet so it can go right into Lake Huron, which is 21 feet lower than Lake Superior.

On this day, there were two ships ahead of us, and John Crum and I were on the dock moving cables while a third man turned the winch, which wound up the cables and moved the ship forward. It was a cold winter day with a strong wind buffeting us. We were standing between the two ships, and there was about thirty feet of open water between us. We were freezing. I was standing behind John when I heard a loud screech. I found out a cable detached from the onshore spile and came swinging across the dock, and hit John and me. It hit so hard that we flew into the 36° water below. When I hit the surface, I landed on my back with John on top of me. The next thing I knew, I looked up and Ivan was standing on the dock, yelling to me to wrap the heaving lines around John and myself. I was able to get two heaving lines around us, and Boris and about six other fellas on the deck pulled us out of the water. John Crum was unconscious, with blood all over the front of his chest. Ivan had an ambulance come and pick us up.

At the hospital, a doctor told me I'd cracked two ribs. He taped me up to a point where I could hardly breathe, so the ribs wouldn't come apart and could heal properly. I'd have to keep taped up for at least two weeks, but a short time later I was released from the hospital. I immediately went to see how John was doing.

I saw Ivan in the emergency room, and he told me I was very lucky, but John was in critical condition. The cable had crushed his chest, broken three ribs on his right side and punctured his lung. Our ship had gone on to Buffalo, New York but they would pick us up on their way back here at the Sioux locks.

Later, I was talking to a young pretty nurse about what happened and I mentioned I would have to stay here for about a week until my ship picks me up. I asked her where I could find a motel, she said, "I'll be right back." I thought she was going to find out where the closest motel was, but when she came back she told me that she lives with her aunt and uncle who have a large home in town. "I told them about what happened to you and asked if they could put you up for a week, they said bring him home we are glad to help out."

"Thank you, but I don't want to inconvenience anyone."

"It's no problem, it's a very large home with six bedrooms, and because they are very old they put their bedroom on the first floor so they wouldn't have to climb the stairs. I have one bedroom and a friend who is a nurse here has a bedroom, so you have your pick of any of the other four bedrooms." She gave me the address and told me how to get to the house, and when I returned to the waiting room, Ivan was there with John's wife and two sons. John was still in critical condition. I told Ivan about the young nurse, Ivan replied that he would find a place for himself and John's wife and boys so they won't have to drive back and forth from their home to the hospital.

The nurse's house was like a mansion. I picked out a nice room, took a shower, went to sleep, and didn't wake up for 12 hours. That evening, I met up with the pretty nurse. Her name was Marie, and her friend, who also lived in the mansion, was Gail. I took them out to dinner and then we returned to the mansion where I met Marie's Aunt and Uncle. We all sat and listen to three radio shows: Amos and Andy, Jack Benny and Fibber McGee and Molly. They were great shows. I remember my mother liked to listen to the same shows, when me and the two girls went up to our rooms, Marie said, "I'll see you later." I didn't know what that meant, but about an hour after I was in bed Marie came to my room. She was stark naked and jumped in bed with me. I was thrilled, but the evening didn't turn out as I expected. I was moaning, not from pleasure, but every time I moved I felt like someone was punching me in the ribs.

The next day, I saw John in a private room. He shook my hand and said, "I guess I'm lucky to be alive and I'm thankful you didn't get hurt too bad. The doctor told me I won't be going back to work for some time, and if I go back to work it will have to be light duty because I lost one of my lungs and the doctors aren't sure whether the other one will fully recover."

After I left John's room, I went down to the hospital cafeteria where I ran into Marie and Gail having lunch. They wouldn't see me for a couple of days because they were working 12 hour shifts Thursday and Friday, but they would see me Saturday night. Again, I wasn't sure what they meant by "seeing" me. I visited John twice a day for the next two days and I thought he was making a rapid recovery. Saturday afternoon, I visited John in his room and he was up walking around with his wife and two boys. A little later, an orderly came in with a wheelchair and said he had to take John down for a chest x-ray, but that he should be back in about an hour. While I sat in John's room, Martha, John's wife, told me, "Ivan has been wonderful, I don't know what we could've done without him. He said he talked with the captain, and John will be paid till the end of the season and will also get his end of the year bonus. Ivan helped me apply for Social Security disability for John, and also put in a workers compensation claim. He submitted a copy of the accident report and included a statement that the Oglebay Norton Co, that owns the ship will not contest John's claim. Ivan thinks John will receive total compensation, and should receive a monthly check for the rest of his life. It looks like we're going to be all right!" I left the room with a good feeling that it's a good thing Ivan was there to help out.

Saturday evening, I once again took the girls out to dinner, which was the least I could do since Marie's aunt and uncle would not take any money for letting me stay at the house. After dinner, Marie said Gail and I are going shopping and will be back by nine and will see you then. I went to the hospital and visited John and Ivan. John told me he would be going home Monday. Ivan alerted me that our ship will be at the Sioux locks Tuesday evening between six and ten. "I'll take care of both you and John's hospital bill, and the company will reimburse me."

When I got to the mansion, Marie's aunt and uncle said the girls are home from shopping, and they're waiting for you upstairs. When I walked into my room, both Marie and Gail were stark naked on my bed. Marie said,

"You're late so we started without you!" I couldn't believe what I was seeing, these two girls were making love. "Come on get undressed and join us!" But I didn't join them, I just sat back and watched. When I got back aboard the ship, I told Jack Talbot all about my trip to the hospital, and especially about Marie and Gail. Jack Talbot laughed and said, "Marie is double gated," I asked Jack what he meant by that, he said, "she swings both ways, she likes boys and girls," and he laughed.

## LEAVING THE SHIP

It was December 1st when our ship pulled into the bay outside of Lackawanna, New York. The lake was frozen over around the docks, but this was where our ship planned to lay over for the winter. We had to wait till the icebreakers opened up the channel and cleared the ice away from the docks. On December 7th, we finally tied up at the Lackawanna dock.

I called the YMCA in East Cleveland to tell Mr. Cumler, the director of the Y, that I was coming home by train. Mr. Cumler told me that Cleveland was having the worst snowstorm that they had seen in 40 years. He told me to call him when the train got into the terminal and he would see if he could find someone with a four-wheel-drive vehicle to take me to the Y House.

Jack Talbot, Donnie Hudson, and Danny O'Brien came by to say goodbye. Jack Talbot told me that Ivan had called a cab to take me to the train terminal and the cab would be there in about a half hour. Donnie Hudson said he would call me because he only lived about 10 miles from my house, and maybe we would go for another plane ride. Danny O'Brien handed me an envelope; it was an invitation to his wedding and the reception. He was getting married on February 15th at St. John's Cathedral in downtown Cleveland. "I'll be there," I said.

When I went out on the dock to look for the cab, Boris, Izzie, and Jim Robertson were there standing on the ship's deck behind me. All three of them yelled "Bill Kilius!"

When I turned around, Boris had a rope in his hand and was lowering a basket down to me. Izzie said, "The cook helped us make a picnic basket for you." Jim said, "That's in case you get hungry on the train."

I thanked them. "I'll miss you guys. Especially listening to your music." Izzie replied, "If we ever get around to making a record, we will be sure to send you a copy." Boris added, "Promise me you won't give that basket away."

I promised I wouldn't. The cab was there, so I waved goodbye and got in the cab heading for the train terminal.

As I sat in the cab, the first thing that came to my mind was that Ivan didn't say goodbye. When I got to the train terminal, I was going to pay the cab driver, but he told me that before he picked me up, an old man stopped him and paid my cab fare plus a good tip. "He gave me an envelope and told me to make sure you get it," the cab driver explained. He handed me the envelope and I tucked it into the basket, then left for the the train terminal.

When I was aboard the train and comfortably seated, I opened the basket to get Ivan's letter, but I was distracted by something rolled up in a dish towel. I opened the towel, and there was the knife that Boris had stolen from my locker. I suppose Boris was a decent person after all.

After that, I opened Ivan's letterHe wrote:

*"I don't like saying goodbye, so I wrote you a letter instead."*

*"I have to tell you what our captain told me: 'I pray Bill Kilius isn't thinking about coming back to work for us next season. Four times I thought he was going to kill himself, diving off the ship, riding the lifeline, almost going off the Toledo dock with the cable, and jumping into the hole filled with grain, I think he's accident-prone, and my heart can't take having Bill Kilius on our ship for another season.' I told the captain that you plan to go to college with the intention of eventually becoming a YMCA executive. The captain felt that was a great idea and wished you the best of luck.*

*I think the YMCA is a great institution and I've seen the excellent work they do with the youth in Detroit's inner-city. The only thing I see wrong with the YMCA is they don't pay their employees enough money to make a decent living, especially if you want to get married and have children. Now if you're single, that's a different story. Think about doing volunteer work for the Y if you plan to have a family.*

I'm enclosing the number of my mailbox in Windsor, Canada, if you would drop me a line from time to time, I'm interested in seeing how your life progresses.

Sincerely,
Ivan Kennedy

PS: John Crum would like to hear from you, so I also included his address."

# BOOK 3

## ON THE PSYCHIATRIC WARD

Portsmouth Naval Hospital (Now Naval Medical Center Portsmouth)

## ON THE PSYCHIATRIC WARD

During the time of the Korean War, the United States began to draft young men my age into the Army. I desperately didn't want to be drafted. My stepfather was a "professional" Army man and we had lived in different military camps all over the country. Sometimes we had to eat "Army chow." Combined with all the marching, it didn't interest me, but I knew for sure that I would pass the physical.

Since I had sailed on the Great Lakes as a deckhand, traveling from port to port and seeing different cities, I

116

knew I preferred the water. Plus the food in the Navy was excellent, and I enjoyed the outdoors. A friend of mine, Jerry Friedlander, had three brothers in the Navy who made it sound very appealing.

So, Jerry and I enlisted and not long after we were sent to the United States Naval Training Center in Bainbridge, Maryland, to start serving.

My first few weeks in boot camp were enjoyable. There were sixty young men in our company. Our company commander was a Chief Petty Officer named Alex Johnson, who was a good person. Chief Johnson knew my background; I had worked part time at the Y.M.C.A. for a number of years, and was a certified aquatics instructor both at the Y.M.C.A. and in the American Red Cross. Chief Johnson assigned me to coach the swimming team. Each company had its own team and would compete with other companies. We were fortunate to have some good swimmers, and because of that, we won every meet.

When I was halfway through boot camp, Chief Johnson came to me with a proposition. He said that four chiefs had been reassigned to the pool in our field house, but they had no aquatic background. They were put in charge of teaching recruits how to swim and how to jump off a thirty-four-foot platform tower. All sailors have to know how to jump in case they ever have to jump off of a sinking ship, but there is a certain way you have to jump so that you won't injure yourself. I had already helped two boys in our company overcome their fears of jumping, and Chief Johnson said if I would help out at the pool, I would not have to attend any of the morning classes. Instead, I would work at the pool from 9:00 a.m. to 11:45 a.m. Then, I would come back to the barracks and go to lunch with my company. I found the morning classes to be tortuous, so I agreed to take the new assignment.

The four chiefs at the pool were pleased and they let me run the program. In fact, most of the time they were playing cards. About a week later, the chiefs awarded me with a weekend of shore patrol duty in Wilmington, Delaware.

While I was on duty in downtown Wilmington, two policemen were dragging an old man out of a bar. Each policeman had a leg, and the man's head was bouncing off the floor.

I stopped them and said, "That's no way to treat a person!" They told me to mind my own business and get out of the way and they started pulling the man again.

I hit the policeman's arm with my billy club and I told him to stop. The two policemen did stop and then went immediately to their patrol car and called my supervisor.

He came and told me I was out of line because the situation was a civil matter. The supervisor said he was so upset with me that he was sending me back to camp. Chief Johnson didn't reprimand me, but he said, "We better keep you here at camp."

A week later, I was in trouble again. The chiefs were supposed to let me know when it was 11:45 AM so I could go back to the barracks and go to lunch with my company. There is a rule that recruits must go to lunch with their companies. I went up to the four chiefs and said, "It's 12:15 now. I'm going to miss lunch."

They said they were sorry and that I should go to lunch. They also said that if anybody stopped me, to tell them they had told me to jump in behind any company that was going to lunch. I didn't want any trouble, so I went back to my barracks and Chief Johnson was eating his lunch that his wife had prepared. I told him what had happened at the drill hall and he said, "I'm giving you an order to go to lunch. If anybody stops you, tell them I gave you an order to fall in behind any company that's going to lunch." So I did as instructed, and as soon as I saw a company, I jumped in behind them. Unfortunately, a Lieutenant "J.G." stopped me and said, "You're a straggler and I want you to stand over against the backstop with your nose touching the wall." Then the lieutenant walked away.

When he caught four other recruits straggling, he told us we should chain step down to the end of the grinder and back. Chain step is where you have to stand so close to the person in front of you that your stomach is touching their back. I felt that chain stepping is a disgusting, degrading, and embarrassing type of punishment. I pleaded to the lieutenant to let me explain.

"Keep your mouth shut and do as you're told." I didn't move. The lieutenant had the four other recruits sit down. Then he came back to me and said, "You dumb ass son of a bitch. Don't you understand English?" "I would like to explain…" The lieutenant pushed me and said, "Get in line." "Don't push me." I said. Then the lieutenant, with both hands, shoved me back a couple of steps. I hit him so hard in the jaw that his feet went off the ground and he landed on his back. I looked around and realized there were four shore patrol guards standing around me. I had to follow them to the brig.

I stayed a night in the brig, and the next morning, Chief Johnson came and we went back to the barracks. He let me call my stepfather, who was a captain in the Army. I talked to my father and he advised, "It sounds like you're going to be court-martialed. If this is so, I'll get you a military lawyer. It's most important that you get a statement from the four chiefs saying that they gave you permission or instructed you to straggle to lunch. And have your company chief give a statement that he ordered you to straggle as well to the chow hall. It is also important that you write out a statement that you were given orders to be where you were and that the lieutenant put his hands on you twice."

A few days later, I was ordered to appear before five officers, who may have been classified as judges for this hearing. They had statements from the four chiefs and my company commander. They said, "We've talked this over. We are going to give you a COG." I asked what a COG was, and they said it's a discharge called "Convenience Of the Government."

I told them, "I don't want to be discharged. I joined the Navy to serve my country, and if I have to serve it in the brig, so be it." I also told them my father was a captain in the Army and that he had instructed me to get a military lawyer to plead my case. The panel of judges said they would get back to me. The next day, one of the judges informed me I was to remain in the Navy, but I would have to go through boot camp again.

I did as I was instructed and when I completed boot camp, the same judge came to me. He asked me, "if you had your choice, what kind of duty would you like?" "Sea duty. I sailed on the Great Lakes and I enjoyed the work." Then he asked me, "What kind of work would you not want?" Of course, being naïve, I said, "I don't want to be a bedpan jockey."

The next day, I was given my orders. I was to go to Portsmouth, Virginia to the Naval Hospital and start corpsman school.

After graduating from corpsman school, I asked for sea duty. Later, I was told I had two choices: the highly contagious, spinal meningitis ward, or the neuropsychiatric service working with the criminally insane. I didn't hesitate. I took the assignment to work on the neuropsychiatric ward.

My stepfather told me he was almost positive that the judges had written and submitted in my portfolio that I was never to be granted sea duty.

## DR. KELLY AND THE BAR IN NORFOLK

Dr. Kelly was a psychiatrist who worked in the neuropsychiatric service with his wife, an attending nurse. One evening, Dr. Kelly received a call from a doctor in Norfolk, Virginia who informed him that there was a Marine in a downtown bar thought to be insane. Apparently, the Marine had two broken bottles, one in each hand, and had cut a shore patrol officer while screaming obscenities.

The shore patrol and the local police had already evacuated the bar and had the Marine locked inside. The Norfolk doctor told Dr. Kelly that he thought the Marine should be brought to the neuropsychiatric service. Dr. Kelly agreed and informed the doctor that he would send an ambulance with three men and bring the Marine back to the neuropsychiatric service.

Dr. Kelly told three of us to take an ambulance with mattress, a straitjacket, and shackles, and see if we could restrain the Marine and safely bring him to a locked cell.

The three corpsmen Dr. Kelly sent were Lou Derubes, who was a heavyweight wrestler in high school, Carl Argenzio, who was a short, overweight, out-of-shape guy, and myself. We had been taught how to restrain a patient without hurting them, but in this case, we weren't so sure of ourselves because the Marine in question was armed and dangerous.

As we were driving to the bar, Lou and I decided the best way to restrain the Marine was to rush him with the mattress and pin him. Then we would pull his legs out from under him and cross his legs, flipping him over, keeping the mattress on top of him. Then we would attempt to take the bottles out of his hands. We would have to shackle his legs so he couldn't kick us. Then we could put the straitjacket on him.

We could see Carl was terrified, so we told him that he would be responsible for bringing the straitjacket and shackles to us once we had the Marine down with the mattress on top of him.

When we got to the bar in Norfolk, there was a large crowd outside, waiting to see how we were going to handle the situation. Lou and I wondered out loud why the shore patrol or the police had not shot the Marine. We found out later that the doctor who called had informed the police and shore patrol that he needed to immediately be evaluated and treated for mental illness.

As we walked into the bar, the first thing we noticed was that the Marine was a big fellow, easily six feet tall and well over two hundred pounds. Fortunately, his back was against the wall, which was to our advantage. We could keep him between the mattress and the wall and slide him down the wall.

We were lucky. Everything went as planned. Lou and I were able to get the bottles out of his hands without getting cut. We had his legs shackled, but the toughest part was getting him into the straitjacket.

As we walked out carrying the Marine, the crowd cheered. We placed him in the back of the ambulance and stayed with him to see that he didn't hurt himself. On the way back, we let Carl drive the ambulance.

Dr. Kelly was waiting for us back at the neuropsychiatric ward. We carried the Marine to a cell, an eight by ten foot room with heavy gauge screen on the window and door, the kind you couldn't even break with an axe.

Dr. Kelly told us to hold the Marine down, and he gave him a shot which knocked him out. Dr. Kelly said, "We will wait an hour to make sure he's out, and then we will remove the shackles and straitjacket."

After we administered the shot, Carl pulled Dr. Kelly aside. Still white as a ghost, he asked to be transferred from the neuropsychiatric service. Dr. Kelly thought it was a good idea, and approved the transfer. After that, Lou and I became lifelong friends.

## GIZZARD

Gizzard was a first-class seaman, with over ten years of experience in the Navy. Six of those years were spent working in the neuropsychiatric service.

Gizzard was not well liked by the other enlisted personnel. He enjoyed showing his rank, degrading and reprimanding us in front of the doctors. At other times, he was petty. He would say things like, "You're out of uniform! Your pants are a half-inch too short."

Gizzard would walk with the doctors when they made their rounds. It made us sick to watch Gizzard play up to the doctors. I recall one staff member remark that she was waiting for him to drop to the floor and lick their shoes.

Worse, he would also make sarcastic remarks to the patients. He especially enjoyed tormenting Dobo, the patient we brought in from the Norfolk bar. Dobo and Gizzard had an ongoing verbal war. Gizzard would usually win by saying, "Well, I'm here, and you're on your way to prison." Dobo hated Gizzard, and for good reason.

One day, we had an order from Dobo's doctor to give him a hydrotherapy treatment. Hydrotherapy is the use of water to treat a patient who has some type of disease, and is also generally used for restoring good health. It's very relaxing, and the doctors in our ward believed it could help control a patient's behavior.

Gizzard was working the controls of the hot tub. After we shackled Dobo into the tub, Gizzard started with warm water, then turned on the jets. Just as Dobo was completely relaxed, Gizzard spun the control wheel to the left and dropped the water temperature from one hundred four degrees down to fifty degrees. The water was freezing, Dobo started swearing and squirming against his chains. Gizzard started laughing and acting like he was driving a racecar.

Some of the staff thought Gizzard was funny. I disagreed. I thought Dobo might have a heart attack. It took four of us to bring Dobo into the hydro room and place him into the large tub, but it only took two of us to help him back to his cell. He was so weak he could hardly stand.

I have to admit, after the incident with hydrotherapy, Dobo was more cooperative. When he was released from the neuropsychiatric service and then taken into custody to stand trial, he told Gizzard, "I'll be back to get you. No matter how long I'm in the brig, I won't forget you."

About a year later, I heard from a secretary that Dobo had been given a dishonorable discharge and was to be released that day. After I heard that, I ran out to the pay phone in the lobby and called our office to ask for Gizzard. I remembered how Dobo talked, using words like, "dees,", "dems," and "dose." When Gizzard came to the phone, I said, "You know who dis is. I'm coming to get you." I hung up and then ran back to the office, where Gizzard was still holding the phone, pale as a ghost. He dropped the phone and ran into Dr. Kelly's office.

About a half hour later, Dr. Kelly called me into his office. He told me how Gizzard had come asking for protection for him and his wife. Dr. Kelly was sharp enough to know Dobo wasn't going to come to Virginia from the Bronx just to get even with Gizzard.

I wasn't sure how Dr. Kelly would take it, but I told him the whole story, starting back when Dobo first came to the neuropsychiatric service to when he told Gizzard he was going to come back and get him. Dr. Kelly laughed and said, "I'll convince Gizzard that Dobo is not going to come for him, but please don't mention to anyone that you made the phone call."

Dr. Kelly was a great guy, and the staff all enjoyed working with him. Quite unlike Gizzard, who, after a few days, went back to being his old nasty self.

## A SAD CASE

Jim Marinelli was a forty-seven-year-old Naval officer who had one more year to go. He would have retired with thirty years of active service.

He was brought into our ward with symptoms of memory loss and difficulty thinking. What initially struck me about Jim Marinelli was that he had no living relatives. All his friends were in the military service. When they came to see him, they would all say he was a great person and they were sad about losing him.

Jim was tested and interviewed so the doctors could determine what his problem was. Later, the doctors diagnosed him with an incurable form of dementia. We would have to find a place that could take care of him. I told Dr. Kelly that I thought Jim was too young to have dementia, but Dr. Kelly replied he had seen it happen to even younger men.

Jim was not a problem on the ward. I guess it was because Jim was aware that he had memory problems. He would say, "I'm really losing it, and if I get any worse, I won't know who I am." We tried to cheer him up by saying, "You're going to be okay." But the doctors kept telling us that he was going to get much worse, to the point where he would need round-the-clock care and attention. The doctors' plan was to get him into a veterans' home in Richmond, Virginia.

One of the sad things about working on the neuropsychiatric service was working with a patient who you knew was not going to improve. Thank God it seldom happened that way.

## MACLOUD

One late afternoon, Dr. Kelly called Gizzard and me into his office and said a call came through about a young Marine who had gone crazy.

The man in question had driven up to the entrance of the Norfolk, Virginia shipyard. He showed the guard his ID and said he had brought his girlfriend to show her the ship he worked on. The guard could see that they were both drunk. The guard said, "Just a minute. I have to go into the guard house and check on something."

As soon as the guard turned around, the Marine sped off into the shipyard. The gate guard sent a patrol in pursuit, and the marine apparently told his girlfriend to get out of the car, and then took off. He hit three parked cars and damaged his own in the process. The exit leading out of the shipyard was locked, so he crashed right through the gate, slamming metal through his front windshield.

The patrol somehow lost the Marine in traffic, but with a description of the car and the license plate number they were able to determine that the vehicle belonged to Tim Macloud, an eighteen-year-old Marine stationed in Norfolk.

The police were able to get ahold of the young Marine's supervisor. They learned that Tim Macloud had an excellent record. His superiors wanted him in custody and treated at a hospital with a psychiatric unit.

Hours later, the police got a report from a lady claiming that a young Marine with an injured right hand had come in the front door of her house, ran through the house and out the back door into the woods known as "Dismal Swamp" behind her house. A short time later, the police found Macloud's car, out of gas on the side of the road.

Dr. Kelly told Gizzard and me to take an ambulance and go to the lady's house where Macloud was last seen. He said to go to the back of the house and see if we could find him, then bring him back and place him into a locked ward.

When Gizzard and I got to the address, we went to the back yard. The lady showed us where Macloud had gone in. Gizzard said to me, "Go in there and see if you can find him."

I peered into the woods and then back at Gizzard like I thought he was crazy. He was unfazed, "I'm giving you an order, and if you don't do as I say, I'm putting you on report."

I told him there were alligators, poisonous snakes, wild animals, quicksand, and that there are over twenty-six thousand acres of wetlands and forest. I said, "We could get lost in there. If you want to go in with me, we should first get a compass and then wait till morning to go in."

"Fine. I'm reporting you." He called Dr. Kelly. Moments after the phone conversation, he said, "Let's just drive around the edge of the swamp and maybe we will see Macloud when he comes out." Gizzard did not say any more about me going into the swamp or that I was on report. It was obvious that Dr. Kelly had straightened him out.

The next morning, we received a call from the local police that Macloud had turned himself in and was being treated at a local hospital. The police said they would hold Macloud until we came and picked him up.

Two daytime staff members retrieved him the next morning. When I arrived later in that day, I was told that Macloud was sleeping. He had cut off the first joint of a finger on his right hand. He was a mess. We let him shower and gave him pajamas. He looked embarrassed and exhausted.

Macloud slept for twenty-four hours. After he was awake for a while, I asked him to tell me what he remembered about the incident that got him into all this trouble.

"It all started last Friday when I received a seventy-two hour pass. I was in a bar in Norfolk having a beer, when I met a young lady. I bought her a drink called a tequila sunrise. I started drinking the tequila sunrises with her. I kept thinking that I hadn't eaten anything all day and I should eat something, but it never happened. I got to the bar about two in the afternoon, and I can't remember even leaving the bar."

When I asked him the name of the bar, he couldn't remember. I also asked him about the girl. He couldn't even tell me her name.

I stopped asking questions, and told him what I knew about the incident. He looked pale. "I don't remember leaving the bar. The next thing I remember was standing in warm water up to my knees and it was very dark. I walked till I found a dry spot where there were some large trees. I stayed there till daylight. I climbed one of the trees but I didn't recognize anything but woods and swamp. I did hear what sounded like a large truck on the move. I started walking in the direction of the sound. When I found the road, I started walking till I found a police station and I turned myself in. Later, an ambulance came and brought me here." He looked at me, earnestly.

"All I know is I'm in trouble. I'm an American Indian and I have two older brothers who are also in the Marines. I love being a Marine, and it sounds like I'm going to the brig and then I'll be given a dishonorable discharge." He looked like he was ready to cry. I told him I wasn't sure what the outcome would be, but to please work with the doctors and they would find out the reason all this happened.

After a month of counseling, Dr. Kelly determined that Macloud suffered from acute alcohol poisoning which can be extremely dangerous. The symptoms are seizures, blackouts, amnesia, or mental confusion. Macloud told Dr. Kelly that the most he ever drank at one time was three beers, and tequila sunrises tasted like you were drinking pop.

Dr. Kelly told Macloud that one tequila sunrise drink had more alcohol in it than three beers. He said, "You don't know how much your system can handle before you have a reaction, so the safest thing is not to take in any alcohol."

## DONNY SKIDDARYS

Donny Skiddarys was one of the few patients admitted to the locked ward on the neuropsychiatric center who didn't have criminal charges pending. He had to spend thirty days in the brig for disobeying an order. While in the brig, he was treated for a bleeding ulcer.

We had heard that Donny was placed in the locked ward until his ulcer was under control, and then he was going to be released from the Navy and given a "convenience of the government" discharge because he could not adjust to military life.

Donny was somewhat of a clown. He was always happy and could tell jokes for hours. One day, Donny was standing at the window trying to talk to people passing by, but nobody would answer him. Don Norris, one of our staff members, told Donny that the staff were instructed to never converse with patients from the neuropsychiatric service. Donny laughed and said, "That's great!"

Later, he started yelling at the people passing by the window, especially the officers. He would say things like,

"Hey, ugly! You should wear that hat pulled over your face because you're so ugly!"

Then the other patients on the ward started doing the same thing. They thought it was funny. The windows had a heavy gauge screen on the inside to prevent them from breaching the glass, so the people passing by couldn't see who was talking to them.

When Dr. Kelly found out what the patients were doing, he announced to the staff that if we couldn't put a stop to this behavior, he would have the windows closed on the street side. This would stop our patients harassing the people passing by, but we also didn't have air conditioning. With all the windows open, we at least had a nice breeze coming through the ward.

Donny told us later it was his fault. He apologized and said he would talk to the patients and get them to stop harassing people walking by. Donny talked to the patient's and for some reason, they listened to him. I guess because they all knew he was a little crazy.

Don Norris became close friends with Donny. One night, when he was giving out medications to patients, Donny said, "Give me a swig of that chloral hydrate and maybe I'll get some sleep tonight!"

Norris handed the bottle to Donny and Donny took a large drink. I would guess he drank about four to six ounces of chloral hydrate. When I saw how much he drank, I called Norris and Donny aside and said, "You drank too much and if we don't do something right away, Donny, you'll be dead from respiratory arrest!"

They were both in shock.

I called a corpsman friend who worked in the emergency room at the hospital, and he came right over with a stomach pump. We used it on Donny.

The emergency room corpsman said we would have to keep Donny awake and walking around and give him lots of coffee. Donny and Norris were lucky the treatment worked, and only the four of us knew about the incident.

A few nights later, Don Norris and I decided to switch our schedules around. This was in the summer, and we asked for night duty so that one of us would sleep half the night and the other one would sleep the second half. We had planned to spend the days at Virginia Beach body surfing, and in theory we wouldn't have to go home and sleep before going to the beach.

But we ran into a problem, which never happened to us before; nobody had ever come to the ward to check on us before.

The first night, a young lieutenant came into the ward and said he would stop in about every two hours and check on us. He also said he would be working nights all month. This meant we wouldn't be getting much sleep.

On the second night when the lieutenant came into the ward, Donny came running across the room and jumped on the lieutenant, knocking him down. He rolled around on top of the lieutenant. I tried to stop Donny. Norris wasn't helping.

When I finally pulled Donny off the lieutenant, Norris and I carried Donny and placed him in a cell, a small empty room with heavy gauge screens on the door and windows. We then went back and helped the lieutenant up. He was sitting on the floor in shock. When he finally recovered, he apologized for disturbing us and that from now on he would stop at the outside window by our office to check on us.

Later, I went and checked on Donny to make sure he was okay. As I was about to leave, he whispered to me, "Don't forget the pizza and two beers." I walked back out to Norris and said, "What's Donny's talking about?"

"Oh. Donny and I staged this whole thing to keep the lieutenant from coming in and checking on us. I promised Donny I would give him a large pizza and two beers."

That night, I had my wife pick up a large pizza and two beers, and bring them to us. We let Donny sit in his cell and have his pizza and beer.

For the rest of the summer, we got our rest without any interruptions from the young Lieutenant.

## JANE THOMAS

Jane Thomas was Dr. Kelly and Dr. Perless' secretary. She was from Missoula, Montana. After high school, she attended the University of Montana for two years, majoring in English and American History.

Her boyfriend, who was also her childhood sweetheart, was to be drafted because of the Korean conflict, so she decided to join the US Navy. Three months later, Jane joined the Navy as a Wave (at the time women in the Navy were called Waves). She and her boyfriend thought they were going to be stationed together, but it didn't work out that way. His home base was San Diego, California, and hers was Portsmouth, Virginia.

They stayed in close contact with each other by phone and mail. When they were on their last leave together, they got engaged. At that point, her fiancé's father gave them a large piece of land on Flathead Lake in Montana—one of the cleanest lakes in the world, close to Glacier Park.

The two of them planned to run a fishing camp. She would teach school in the winter months, and in the summer, she would help her husband run the camp during peak season. Flathead Lake is a fisherman's dream, with over one hundred eighty-five miles of shoreline and two hundred miles of water containing lake trout, yellow perch, and whitefish.

Jane was an amazing person. In addition to being an excellent secretary, while in the Navy, she took enough correspondence courses from the University of Maryland to earn herself a Bachelor of Science degree. She also had a hobby of doing research and attending conferences and lectures on American Indians. Dr. Kelly once said that she was an authority on the American Indian.

When Jane found out about Tim Macloud, who was not only American Indian but was from her hometown of Missoula, Montana, she started to visit Tim after work. I think they became good friends.

Tim said Jane was a fantastic person. She knew more about his Indian heritage than he did. Jane and her fiancé had visited his reservation on the Flathead River a number of times.

One day, I was having lunch with Jane, and she said to me, "Do you know that Tim Macloud is a very honorable and conscientious person? And what's sad is, it appears he's going to be found guilty and sentenced to no less than two years at the federal penitentiary in Fort Leavenworth, Kansas." She took a moment to look right at me, "Do you think there's anything you can do for him?" I said, "I'm working on it." "That's what I wanted to hear."

About a month later, Dr. Kelly received a call from Jane's roommate, who was supposed to be gone for the weekend visiting Myrtle Beach, South Carolina, but came home because of poor weather. When Jane's roommate walked into their apartment, she found Jane in the bathtub. She had cut her wrists. The roommate immediately called the rescue squad, but they were unable to save her.

There was a telegram on the table from her fiancé's family saying there was a terrible accident and her fiancé was killed. Later, we found out that her fiancé was driving on a divided highway, and an old lady pulled out in front of a truck carrying a full load of stone. When the driver swerved to miss the old lady, his axle broke, sending his truck into oncoming traffic. The truck hit Jane's fiancé's car head-on and he was killed instantly.

Jane's body was sent back to Missoula to be buried. Dr. Kelly and Dr. Perless flew to Missoula to attend the funeral. When I told Tim Macloud about Jane's death, he said, "Jane just wanted to join her man in the next life." I didn't say anything, but I thought, "Maybe he knows something I don't."

Life is so strange how things can change. One day, she has everything to live for. The next, she commits suicide.

# THE CHATTERBOX

One Saturday morning, I came to the ward to relieve Don Norris from night duty. Don told me he'd had a bad night. He said, "Last night at about 11:45 p.m., three Marines carried in a fellow Marine who was totally out of it. They said he started screaming and swearing at a person he saw, but there was nobody there. I had them take the fella and put him in the locked cell, after removing his shoes, his belt, his shirt, and his tie."

The Marines said his name was Terry Trimore. About a week before, Terry left to go on a thirty-day leave. He was gone for about five days, but then he came back to the barracks.

Terry had told the Marines that when he got home, his wife and two kids were gone. There was a note on the table from his wife saying she went back to Cincinnati to live with her mother and she was filing for divorce. He was so shook up; he didn't see it coming.

Terry started drinking and didn't stop. When he finally sobered up, it was five days later. He decided to return to his barracks.

At the barracks, he wasn't drinking, but he was depressed. He had been back two days, when all of a sudden he started acting strange. He stopped talking, which was unusual for Terry, who apparently was always chatting about something. Then, at about eight o'clock, he started screaming and yelling at someone, but there was nobody there.

After dropping Terry off, the Marines said they would inform his commanding officer of what had happened, and left.

I spoke with Donny, who overheard that Terry was still on his thirty days leave, so he wouldn't be classified as going AWOL. Terry had been screaming and yelling all night and could be heard from both locked wards.

I wrote down everything that Donny had told me about Terry Trimore's situation. Then I called Dr. Kelly, who was the on-duty officer even though he was at home. We were told to call him if there was ever a problem on the ward.

Dr. Kelly told me that when a person goes on a heavy drinking spree and then suddenly stops drinking, sometimes they can experience vivid hallucinations, one to three days later. Alcohol abuse can also create a vitamin deficiency and could cause low blood sugar. Finally, he said there was a specific medication proven to be effective in treating alcohol withdrawal. Dr. Kelly said, "We need to get a copy of Terry Trimore's medical records, which can also help us in treating him." I did everything Dr. Kelly said, and fortunately we managed to find him the right medication.

After a couple of days, he was able to be placed with others on the ward. But there was a problem with Terry: he never stopped talking. Often, if nobody was speaking to him, he would butt into other patients' conversations. He seemed very bright and knowledgeable, but it was obvious that the other patients didn't want to hear everything he had to say.

Terry made friends with Gizzard because he agreed with everything Gizzard said. Gizzard was an obnoxious ass, and Terry's closeness with Gizzard made him even less likeable.

A few days later, I came to work and Don Norris said, "We had another problem with Terry Trimore." Don said that Donny Skiddarys had punched Terry because Terry kept butting into Donny's conversations with other patients. Don said, "I hated to do it, but I had to put Donny in a locked cell. Truth is, there've been times when I wanted to punch Terry. He's such a pain in the ass."

Later that night, I told Donny he could come back to the ward. Donny said, "No! Leave me here. If I go back I'm afraid I'll punch Terry again." I told Donny that I would talk to Terry and move his bed to the other end of the ward. Donny returned and fortunately, there were no further problems between the two of them.

I asked Dr. Kelly about why Terry never shuts up. Dr. Kelly laughed and said, "Terry has a personality disorder. I talked to him about it, and he admitted he has two problems he needs to work on: his drinking and he has to learn to listen and not talk so much."

Dr. Kelly said, "You'll be happy to know Terry will be released from the neuropsychiatric service next week, and he will continue to get counseling."

## GARLETTE

Garlette was admitted to the neuropsychiatric ward under the charges of being AWOL, which is "Absent Without Leave." Garlette was rather quiet and withdrawn, and when I was able to read his file, I began to wonder why he ever joined the Marines.

He and his family were devout Catholics. Growing up, he attended different Catholic schools where he was an altar boy, and showed interest in becoming a priest.

After boot camp, Garlette was sent into a war zone, where he and his company were involved in an altercation with enemy troops. While this was going on, some innocent pedestrians were accidentally killed.

When Garlette saw what happened, he became hysterical. He started crying and saying, "I'm going to Hell!" And when he was out of the war zone in a safe area, he disappeared. When they found him, the only thing he would say was, "They are coming after me!"

In Garlette's first two weeks at the ward, he was very cooperative and quiet. The only strange thing I noticed about him was that he took six to ten showers a day.

One rainy day, when we couldn't go out into the courtyard, two of the staff members and two patients were playing pinochle, a four player game.

Garlette came over to me and said, "If you ever need another player, could I please play?" "Do you know how to play pinochle?" "Yes."

The next time we were going to play cards, I invited him to play with us. To our surprise, Garlette was by far the best player of all of us. The only problem we had with Garlette was that he asked if we could take a break while he took a quick shower.

After this happened a number of times, I asked Garlette, "Why do you have to take so many showers?"

He said, "Well, you know, I'm from Mars. If my body is completely covered with sound waves, they will be able to take me back to Mars and punish me for my sins."

"...Go ahead and take a shower. We'll wait for you." Even with the shower thing, we still enjoyed playing cards with Garlette.

I also let the doctors know what Garlette had said. I thought he'd had a mental breakdown because he was so religious and believed so strongly in the Ten Commandments, especially the one that says, "Thou Shalt Not Kill." He must have felt that it was a mortal sin to kill anyone, and he was going to Hell.

Dr. Perless told me, "Garlette is having delusions that he is from Mars. He is convinced that what he believes is true. He also has what is called 'agoraphobia,' which is an intense fear related to being in a situation in which an escape could be difficult. This all may have started because of his extreme depression."

The records reflected that the doctors should try psychotherapy to encourage the patient to acknowledge that his delusions were not real. Unfortunately, this type of treatment was not working with Garlette.

Dr. Perless decided that the only treatment that could bring Garlette out of this delusional state was to have electroshock therapy. To be honest, I thought this type of therapy was archaic, but I knew that it had worked with some people.

The therapy consists of placing two electrodes, one on each side of the patient's head just above the ears, and then sending about 110 volts straight through the brain.

The current only lasts about 3/10 of a second, but can produce a significant seizure or convulsions.

My interpretation of the procedure, from how it was explained to me, is this: it erases all memory, past and present, going back ten years or more. This means the patient will not be able to remember anything that happened in the last ten years. A doctor, with the help of the patient's family and any records they can obtain, can fill in the patient's past in hopes of restoring the patient to a normal life.

Garlette spent several days with Dr. Perless, who was attempting to reconstruct Garlette's life with the hope of minimizing what caused him to fall into such a tragic state of depression. It was also noted that they might need the help of a priest or chaplain when it came to the point where Garlette was involved in the killing of innocent people.

When Garlette came back, he didn't recognize any of the staff. But we were surprised when Garlette asked if he could play pinochle with us. Garlette was only twenty years old, and he couldn't remember much of anything after he turned ten.

"When did he learn to play pinochle?" We asked Dr. Perless. "How does Garlette still remember how to play?" Dr. Perless said he couldn't understand it. He said the brain is a mystery, and we know so little about it.

Later, Garlette was sent to the Philadelphia Naval Hospital to have further treatment. We never found out anything more about him, but we will always remember that he was a remarkable pinochle player, and we prayed that he was able to return to a normal life.

# APPOINTMENT WITH COMMANDER WAGNER

One morning, I was able to get an appointment with Commander Wright Wagner, who was the head of the neuropsychiatric service. He also happened to be a psychoanalyst, and a very brilliant man. I told him, "We have a courtyard for our patients. But all they do is walk around and they barely get any exercise."

I asked the commander if he knew about my background before I entered the Navy. He shook his head as if to say no, he didn't know anything about my past. I told him I worked for the YMCA as a recreation specialist, teaching sports and ran an arts and crafts programs.

The commander thought for moment, "That's interesting. What do you have on your mind?"

"Well, I'd like to set up a program in the courtyard—nothing that could harm the patients or our staff, but something that would give the patients something to do since they have a lot of spare time."

"I'm afraid we don't have any money for that kind of a program."

I shook my head, "It wouldn't cost the neuropsychiatric service anything. I could set up a program on my own."

Commander Wagner looked me up and down, and eventually relented. "Okay, I suppose. As long as it doesn't interfere with your work performance." He gave me a letter with permission to set up a recreation program in our courtyard.

First, I needed the help of a coworker and friend named Lou Darubies. There were twelve picnic tables out in front of the main hospital between the river and the hospital. Lou and I snuck out and dismantled two of the picnic tables and set them up in the neuropsychiatric courtyard.

The courtyard itself was about fifty feet wide and sixty feet long, with a high building on three sides acting as walls. On the fourth side was fifteen-foot-high chain-link fence.

Off base, I'd been doing some volunteer work for the Portsmouth, Virginia Y.M.C.A.. They had a basketball backboard that was broken and was going to be thrown out, so I rescued it from the trash. I was able to get a couple two-by-fours and patch it back together. We set it up over one of the walls in the courtyard. Finally, I bought a basketball. This was the first activity for the patients.

While I was at the Y, I found another piece of equipment they were throwing out, a heavy canvas punching bag with some stuffing hanging out. I applied a little duct tape and covered up the holes, and it worked fine. The problem was, I had nothing to hang the bag from out in the courtyard.

Bobby Wald, a friend and coworker, said, "The bathroom has an empty stall where you could hang the bag. It would be out of the way."

We tried it out, and it worked. To my surprise, some of the patients enjoyed punching the bag. That became the second activity on our ward.

Bobby Wald brought in some paper and colored chalk so the patients could draw. They weren't allowed to have pencils or brushes—some of our more violent inmates might find a way to use them as a weapon.

Another coworker, Donald Norris, brought in a large pad of art paper and some finger paints. As a result, the picnic table was getting a lot of use.

The last project was putting up a volleyball court, I was able to acquire two pieces of pipe, three inches in diameter and twelve feet long, then borrowed a cement drill to make two three-inch holes in the ground that could fit the two pipes so they could stand vertically.

It wasn't much, but the program was a hit. Even the staff began to use the facilities.

## THE GEDUNK WAGON

When the hospital cafeteria closed, a vending company was permitted to come on the grounds and sell snack foods. They came by truck at around 7 PM, selling things like sandwiches, soft drinks, ice cream cakes, and chips. It was called "the Gedunk Wagon."

We walked through the ward making a snack list and collecting money from the patients. We were also permitted to bring one patient to help carry the snacks back to the ward.

If a patient was from a locked ward, one of his arms would be cuffed to the arm of an attending staff member, to prevent the patient from running away. The staff liked the idea of taking a patient because we could just go to the front of the line and say, "We're from the neuropsychiatric service." Not one person could or would protest.

One evening, Norris took the wrong patient to the Gedunk Wagon. When they got to the front of the Wagon, the patient started yelling and grabbing everything in sight and throwing it in our bag. It scared the vendor so badly that he was ready to close up and leave.

The next day, Dr. Perless heard about the incident. He put out an order that patients from the locked ward could not be taken to the Gedunk Wagon, because he felt it was too dangerous to have patients off of the locked ward.

About a week later, when I was working the evening shift, Dr. Kelly called me into his office and said, "Didn't you get the order from Dr. Perless about the Gedunk Wagon?"

"Yes, we did, and we would never disobey Dr. Perless' order."

"Well, Gizzard came to me early today and said that last night you took a patient to the Gedunk Wagon." I smiled.

"I actually took a staff member with a pajama top so we wouldn't have to stand in line for a half hour or more." Dr. Kelly laughed and said, "Go ahead and take a staff member to the Gedunk Wagon, as long as it's a staff member!"

Gizzard lost again.


## THE STRANGE ONE

The only time I ever saw Donny Skiddarys upset was when he came to me and asked if he could move his bed to the other side of the ward.

I told him, "That's not a problem, but why do you want to move your bed?" He said, "You know the new patient that came in last week?" I answered, "Yes, I haven't had a chance to read his file yet."

Donny said bluntly, "He's a strange one." I asked what he meant by that. "His name is Mark Brown and he never talks to anyone. He watches TV all day long and never changes the station, he just watches whatever is on. And I don't think he ever sleeps. He lays on his left side and just stares at me."

"Maybe he likes you," I laughed.

"No, I think he hates me. And I've never done anything to make him hate me. To be honest, he scares me."

"I'll check into it. Meanwhile, move your bed to the front of the ward on the other side. You'll be as far away from him as possible."

Mark Brown was a really good-looking young man. He was twenty-two years old and his file indicated he grew up in an orphanage in Chicago, Illinois. He was an average student, never a discipline problem. He joined the Navy when he was twenty years old, and had gone through boot camp at Great Lakes, Illinois. Eventually, he was stationed aboard a heavy cruiser with well over a thousand sailors.

One day, Mark Brown went through a chief's foot locker that was under the chief's bed. He found a shotgun that the chief had purchased in a foreign country. He took the gun and walked into a room where five chiefs were playing cards. Before they could say anything, Mark Brown aimed the gun right at them and pulled the trigger. It didn't fire, he said, "I knew it wasn't loaded."

Shocked, the chief who owned the gun grabbed it from Mark and said, "You're on report. You have no business going through my footlocker."

About a week before this incident, a sailor had come up missing. It was after the ship had left port, so the sailor must have fallen overboard, jumped, or been pushed over the side.

The chief that owned the gun started wondering about Mark, and if he could have had anything to do with the sailor's disappearance. He checked into the possibility but found out that the sailor and Mark had no visible contact. An investigation team revealed that the sailor was healthy and it was doubtful that the sailor jumped overboard to commit suicide.

The investigative team did not dispense the possibility that Mark Brown may have had something to do with the sailor's disappearance. Because of the incident with the shotgun, they ordered Mark Brown be placed in a locked ward for thirty days for psychiatric observation and evaluation.

When I had the opportunity, I called Mark into my office had him sit down. "Mark, what are your plans for the future?"

"First of all, I'm not crazy. I admit I shouldn't have been teasing the chief with that shotgun: big mistake. As far as my future, I want to stay in the Navy, do my twenty years, take my retirement, and live someplace near the water so I can spend my retirement fishing. That's the only thing I really enjoy." I asked him if he was getting enough sleep.

"I only sleep a few hours a night. It's all I've ever needed and I won't take any medication to make me sleep longer. I don't want to get hooked on drugs."

For the most part, Mark Brown appeared normal, but Dr. Perless told me that he had some serious concerns about him. Unfortunately, the doctor did not elaborate on the subject.

## ANOTHER INCIDENT WITH GIZZARD

After working with Gizzard for almost a year, I realized he never let up on humiliating or harassing the staff members who had to work with him. One morning, Gizzard made a big mistake and left his master key on the admissions desk.

All the staff had a master key to the locked wards and the key was supposed to be with you at all times. Gizzard was always saying, "Where is your key? Show me your key! If I catch you without it, you're on report!"

A staff member, Don Norris, saw Gizzard's key just sitting on the admissions desk and couldn't resist—he grabbed it and immediately ran to me and Lou Daroubies. Gizzard was on the toilet in the staff bathroom, just outside of the locked ward, so we decided to play a trick on him.

Lou moved all the patients from the locked ward out into the courtyard, then Don opened the outside door of the locked ward so it would look like all the patients had escaped.

I went to Gizzard and yelled, "Hey! The outside door to the ward is open! I've got my key!" Gizzard came waddling out in the hall with his pants and underpants around his ankles, frantic. I'm sure he knew he didn't have his master key. When he realized the outside door of the ward was open, he fainted.

Dr. Kelly came down the hall and saw Gizzard lying on the floor with his pants down. We told Dr. Kelly that Gizzard had fainted. I gave Dr. Kelly Gizzard's master key and told him Gizzard had left it on the reception desk.

When Gizzard came to, Dr. Kelly told him, "Here's your key. Everything is alright here, but you don't look so well. I want you to go home and take the rest of the day off. I'll see you in the morning." Gizzard sat, stunned. The doctor repeated, "Everything is alright. There's no problem here."

When Gizzard left, Dr. Kelly called Don, Lou, and me into his office and I explained to him what we had done to Gizzard. I expected him to be angry, but Dr. Kelly only laughed and said, "This stays between the four of us. Also, no more tricks on Gizzard. I'm afraid you're going to kill him."

Lou and I were thankful that Dr. Kelly was on duty when this all went down. From that time on, Gizzard acted more like a normal person and stopped harassing the staff.

## A BIG MISTAKE

Sam Fulton was an eighteen-year-old Marine who claimed to be weak and exhausted. He said he could hardly stand up.
His superiors thought he was faking it, and they placed him in our ward to have him checked out. If he was faking it, he would have to do prison time and would more than likely end up with a dishonorable discharge. His superiors said he had a complete physical when he joined the service and he was in excellent condition.

In reading Sam's record, I saw that he joined the Marines in July and had entered a twelve-week recruit-training program—boot camp, in Paris Island, South Carolina. The records reflected it was an extremely hot summer.

Sam weighed one hundred forty pounds when he joined the Marines. After eleven weeks, he had dropped twenty pounds. This alone was not a good sign. He had endured eleven weeks of rigorous training and at the end of the eleventh week, he told the company commander he could hardly move.

Dr. Kelly gave Sam a number of tests including an electrocardiogram, which proved that Sam's heart was damaged.

Dr. Kelly informed Sam's superiors that, as a result of Sam's tests, Sam would stay on the neuropsychiatric service for six weeks. Then he would be given a medical discharge under honorable conditions.

## A LUCKY BREAK

One evening, most of the patients and the staff were out enjoying the activities in the courtyard, except Macloud who was meeting with Dr. Kelly. The only other people left on the ward were Mark Brown, who was watching TV in the great room, and a Chief Petty Officer who'd been brought in by ambulance the previous night. The Chief had suffered multiple seizures, and was heavily sedated and resting quietly.

When Macloud left Dr. Kelly's office, and went back into the ward, he screamed, "What are you doing?!" Mark Brown was holding a pillow over the chief's face.

Dr. Kelly heard the scream, and so did the staff. At once, we all came running. We grabbed Mark Brown and Dr. Kelly checked the Chief's pulse, "His heart is still beating, but he's unconscious." Mark Brown kept repeating, "I was only adjusting his pillow, I was only adjusting his pillow" as we carried him off to a cell.

Macloud said he was certain about what he saw. The next day, Mark Brown was strapped down, arms, legs and body, onto a cot and then flown to the Philadelphia Naval Hospital, where he would spend the rest of his life in a locked ward; perhaps in isolation.

A few days later, Dr. Kelly called me into his office and said, "We just found out that Macloud stayed here past the day that he was to be turned over to the authorities and set up for a court-martial hearing. Now, because of someone's oversight, Macloud is our responsibility."

"Dr. Kelly, look at it this way. If Macloud had not been here in your office, Mark Brown would have gotten away with murder and probably gone on killing people."

I'm sure Dr. Kelly figured I was the person who buried Macloud's file, so that he would have to remain in the neuropsychiatric service. Now the doctors could decide what kind of a discharge Macloud should receive, or if he should be returned to duty.

About a month later, Macloud was released from the neuropsychiatric service and returned to duty. Macloud was one happy Marine.

I remembered when Jane Thomas had asked me if there was anything I could do for him, when he was facing years of prison.

I told her, "I'm working on it," and I kept my word.

## A NEW PROGRAM

About two months after I started the program in the courtyard, I was called into the survey board. It was my understanding that the only reason the survey board met was to decide whether a patient that had charges against him would be released to the prison authorities, being diagnosed to be of sound mind and able to stand trial, or if the patient was to be sent to the Philadelphia Naval Hospital for further treatment. Other patients would be selected to remain here at this hospital and eventually be given a medical discharge and offered some kind of disability compensation.

I was a nervous wreck because I didn't know what to expect. I thought perhaps someone found out about me taking two picnic tables from the front of the hospital. As I walked to the meeting, Gizzard called over to me, "What did you do now? You know you're in trouble."

In the boardroom, there were six doctors and the head nurse waiting for me, sitting around a long table. Commander Wagner said, "Please have a seat. We have some questions for you." I sat down, and looked up at him.

The Commander began, "As you know, your ward has always been the dirtiest of all of the neuropsychiatric wards. Also, your ward has the most incidents of violence, most sedation given, and a low response to treatment. Now, all of a sudden, your ward is the cleanest of all the wards and has less incidental violence, less sedation given, and most importantly, the patients appear to be responding favorably to treatment. Bill, how do you account for this?"

"I think it's because of the recreation program. We tell the patients that they can't go out into the courtyard till we clean the ward and make the beds. We have between ten and twenty patients, and the ones that are coherent will pitch in to help us clean the ward and make the beds, because they want to go out to the courtyard. As far as less sedation given, which is usually at night, most of the patients are tired and don't need medication to sleep. As far as less violence, the patients are able to release their anger and hostility through exercise. When we see a patient that appears to be hostile or upset, we encourage him to punch the heavy bag and this quite often works. All of the corpsmen that I work with on our ward feel that this program has made their work a lot easier and that the patients are responding better to treatment."

"Bill," the commander said, "all of us here are in agreement that the program you set up is a tremendous success, and it should be a part of all of our programs on the neuropsychiatric service. We were able to come up with the funds, and we want you to run the program on all of the neuropsychiatric wards. You are to be relieved of your present duties and be reassigned as the recreation director of the neuropsychiatric service. You will not have to go to morning roll call. You will start work at 9:00 a.m. and quit at 5:00 p.m. You will not have duty weekends.

You will only answer to us, and the rest of the staff will be notified of your new position. You will also have a parking spot here at the New World psychiatric service."

In a moment, my life changed. I loved so much what I was doing and had such a feeling of accomplishment. And, since I could run the program as I saw fit, there was no pressure from anyone else.

One of our patients had given me a finger painting of two peacocks and it was beautiful. As a way of saying thanks, I gave the picture to Commander Wagner. Later, I saw the picture framed and hanging in his office.

At the end of my tour of duty, Commander Wagner called me in and asked me to reenlist. He said he would promote me as rapidly as possible, and he assured me I would stay with him through my tour of duty.

I asked my stepfather, who was an officer in the Army, if I should accept Commander Wagner's proposition. My stepfather said, "The commander means well, but I don't think he can guarantee everything he's told you."

I thanked Commander Wagner for all he had done for me, but told him I wanted to go on and finish college and eventually work as a full-time Y.M.C.A. executive.

# Book 4
# PAROLE AND PROBATION

## INTRODUCTION

In order for these stories to be told and make any sense, I have to give some of my employment background.

From 1958 to 1964 I worked for the YMCA, where I was involved in their physical fitness program and, eventually, took over the youth department. I was making seven thousand dollars a year; unfortunately, it was barely enough to live on, as I had a family including five children. I enjoyed YMCA work but, in 1964, I was offered a job with a private health club; the starting salary was twelve thousand a year.

I took the job at the health club and I thoroughly enjoyed working with Mr. Stone, the owner. A year later Mr. Stone wanted to retire from the business; he asked me if I wanted to purchase the club. I agreed, and I was able to obtain a loan and buy the club. Because I was paying on the loan, my income was still about $12,000 a year.

One afternoon, Mr. Robert Busby, the physical education director at Cleveland State University, called and asked me if I would be interested in taking the job of aquatic director at Cleveland State University. I knew Mr. Busby because I had worked with him at several swim meets. He told me the job started at $24,000 a year. The only problem was that you can only work at the university for one year if you only have a bachelor's degree.

I took the job at Cleveland State and immediately enrolled at Case Western Reserve University. A year later I received my Master's Degree.

After working at the university for a semester, Mr. Busby called me into his office and said he'd studied my resume. He thought I would be the person to set up a three credit hour course called "Physical Fitness". I agreed to accept the challenge. After attending fitness seminars around the country doing research, I submitted an outline for the course. After a few days, Busby called me into his office and said he was impressed with the course outline I had submitted, but that he would change the course from a three credit hour to a two credit hour. He planned to submit the proposal to the Board of Directors with the recommendation that the course be a requirement for all full-time students.

The Board agreed with Mr. Busby's recommendation; the following semester, I started teaching the course called "Physical Fitness Orientation" along with another course called "Leisure in Our Society". I thoroughly enjoyed teaching both of these courses.

One day I received a letter from a federal judge who was also a member of my health club. He asked me to make an appointment to come and see him because he had a job offer that might interest me. He had talked to three other judges and they agreed with him that this might be a position that I would like. The court had a plan to set up a halfway house in Cleveland; there was no other federal halfway house in the state of Ohio. He said if I was interested I'd have to pick up a course in criminal justice before I could be hired and that, until an approval to build the halfway house could be obtained, they would start me off as a probation officer. The starting salary would be $44,000 a year. I told the judge I was definitely interested and that I would enroll in a criminal justice course or one that was relatively the same. The judge agreed to this and the next day I found a course at Cleveland State that would meet their qualifications.

The very next day I went in to talk to Mr. Busby to tell him about the job the federal judge had offered me. Mr. Busby said, "Hey, that's a $20,000 a year raise! You have to take the job."

After I completed the course, I started work at the Federal Probation Department. But I continued teaching night classes at Cleveland State. As it turned out, for the next 20 years or so, I taught Mondays and Wednesdays from 6 to 10 PM.

Now that I've given my employment background, the stories will begin.

# TWO CROATION WOMEN

One evening I was teaching the physical fitness orientation class. There were 30 students in this class; usually the students' ages ranged from 18 to 22. But, there was one woman who looked around 30 years old. She was beautiful and she was so well dressed she looked like a fashion model. Later, it was obvious to the whole class that she was in amazing physical condition. Her name was Vera Santic and she was very popular with the rest of her classmates.

One night after class I ran into a friend of mine named Ed Keil, a professor of world history at Cleveland State. He came up to me and said, "I see you have Vera Santic in your class." I said, "Yes, and she is an excellent student." He laughed and said, "She's more than just an excellent student. She's an amazing person." I asked, "How's that?" He told me he'd had her in his history class. On the first day of class he told his students that he didn't take attendance and that they'd only have to attend the midterm, finals and the last day of class. No one ever challenged that statement. Vera Santic showed up for the midterm, then for the final and then for the last day. Vera got the highest grade in the class for the midterm and the final!

Ed Keil said he was so curious about her that he

went down to the main office and looked at her file. He was very disappointed to find out that she was married with two children. The file also revealed that she could speak twelve languages and had traveled all over the world. She was truly an amazing person. After Vera Sentic completed my class, regrettably, I never saw her again.

After I had worked in probation for over four years, I was given a strange case. It involved two brothers who were extorting money from Croatian immigrants who had fled from Yugoslavia, which had become a communist country under the rule of the dictator Marshall Tito. The brothers were asking these immigrants and other Croatian people to contribute money to an organization in Europe whose cause was to overthrow Tito and his communist government. The problem came when they threatened people who didn't contribute to their cause. For example, they would tell the communists in Yugoslavia about relatives who were still in Yugoslavia and were plotting against the government. That alone, could cause their family to be killed. What brought the U.S. Federal government into the picture was when the two brothers tried to hijack a plane that was carrying Croatian people who were flying to Yugoslavia to visit their relatives.

The Feds interrogated the two brothers, Boris and Dino, and they admitted their guilt. When asked who else was involved, they said no one in this country. They said they sent all the money they collected to a wine shop in Macedonia. The shop was a wholesale outlet that distributed wine to other countries. The money was sent to the wine distributors but no wine was received. The distributors, in turn, would use the money to try to overthrow the communist government.

The Feds were able to go into Macedonia to investigate the wine shop. They found that the wine shop did exist. But, the day after the two brothers were arrested, it had closed down, leaving no evidence that it was ever there. The Feds thought that Macedonia was a good place to set up an undercover operation: it borders on Greece, Serbia, Bulgaria, and Kosovo. Macedonia is called the "City of Mystery".

After the two brothers were arrested and interrogated, I was instructed to do a presentence report on both of them. Their parents were from Yugoslavia and had come to the U.S. right after Marshall Tito was made president for life in 1963. The family lived in a Croatian neighborhood in the inner city. The father started a moving van business and, when the boys turned 16, they dropped out of school to work with him. Years later, the boys took over the business and they are still in that business today. In checking their prior arrest records, neither of the boys had ever been arrested for anything major, only some minor traffic violations. They were both of average intelligence and were both very strong, probably from doing a lot of lifting on their moving jobs. Boris was 32 years old at the time, married to a woman from Yugoslavia for ten years and had two children. They own their home in a suburb of Cleveland and they attend the same Catholic Church that the boys' parents attended in the inner city. In interviewing the priest from that church, he appeared hesitant to say anything about the brothers. The only thing I could get the priest to talk about was that Boris's wife taught Sunday school and did a phenomenal job. The last part of my presentence report was when I interviewed Boris's wife. I had to wait a week to visit the home and talk with her because she was in Europe visiting her sister. Their home was a small bungalow in a nice neighborhood; it was very clean and adequately furnished. The two children looked healthy and appeared to be well behaved.

When I met Boris's wife I said, "Mrs. Sentic." She said, "Please call me Vi. That's what everyone else calls me." To describe Vi, I would say that she looked like a peasant woman: hair up and covered with a babushka, no makeup or jewelry, wearing a long housedress with an apron, old shoes and ankle socks. I asked her what she knew about her husband's crime. She said, "I know nothing about this arrest situation. I'm from the old country and we women do not pry into our husbands'

162

affairs. Boris never talks to me about what he does outside of the home. He is a good husband and father. We never go hungry, and I'm happy. I love to cook and sew and take care of my family. I go to church and even teach Sunday school. This is my life." She asked me if I would like a cup of coffee and I said,"Yes" even though I don't drink coffee. I had a feeling that I should continue to talk to Vi. I thought there was something definitely wrong with this interview.

Then it came to me; I said to her, "You are Vera Sentic!" She responded with a surprised look on her face. "Yes, I'm Vera Sentic." I said to her, "You don't remember me, but you were in my physical fitness orientation class at Cleveland State University, and I remember you. You can speak twelve languages, and you have traveled all over the world. You are well-educated and highly intelligent, with a fantastic memory." I pointed my finger at her and said, "Vera, you are the head of this organization to overcome Tito and his communist government! Your husband and his brother take orders from you!" Vera's face turned red and she asked if she was under arrest. I said, "No, because your name has never been mentioned in this investigation, and I don't think anyone can prove that you are guilty of anything. But, this information that I discovered today will be in the presentence report, and the government has access to this report. So, they will be keeping their eyes on you. You are smart enough to know that you should not ever become involved in a situation such as this, again." I have to admit I was completely fooled by her appearance and actions. The only reason I knew she was Vera Sentic was that I remembered her name from when I taught her in class at Cleveland State. She was indeed an amazing woman.

It was hard for me to believe that these two women were actually the same person.

## A COMPULSIVE GAMBLER

One of my probationers, Maury Blake, was on probation for three years for income tax evasion. He was also ordered to make restitution for the money he owed the government, which was what he should've paid in income taxes for the two years he didn't file. Maury worked as a driver for Pepsi-Cola. Since I knew the vice president of Pepsi, Jack Karen, I was able to have Jack deduct 10% of Maurice's pay and send it to the federal clerk of courts office. The clerk would credit Maury's restitution account.

The reason Maury didn't file two years income tax forms was because he didn't have the money to pay what he owed. The reason he didn't have the money was because he was a compulsive gambler. So, as another condition to his probation, he was ordered to join Gamblers' Anonymous. I told him, as long as he was on

164

probation, he must attend these meetings. If he stopped attending the meetings, it could be a violation of his probation and he could be sent to prison.

A probation officer usually meets his assigned probationers and parolees once a month. They usually come into the office, but occasionally I would make a home visit. Because Maury worked days, I didn't want him to miss work to come into the office. So I told him I would make a home visit once a month.

On my first home visit I found it very enjoyable. I thought Maury was very fortunate to have a beautiful wife and three lovely children. The home was immaculate and well kept and the children were very well behaved.

At the time, I spent two days a week in the main office (Mondays and Fridays); the other three days I had my office at the Lorain County post office building and I could set my own hours so I could properly work with my caseload. I decided to open my office one evening a week so I could see probationers and parolees that worked during the day. They could report to my office as I instructed. For the next several months, I saw Maury one evening a month at my office. It appeared to me that he was living up to all the conditions of his probation.

Unfortunately, I was mistaken. One morning Maury's wife came to my main office and asked my secretary if she could speak with me. I brought her into my office and sat her down; she started to cry. I asked what was wrong and she said Maury was back gambling and it was worse than ever. Their car was repossessed and they were two months behind in the rent. She was afraid they were going to be evicted. She said she didn't want him arrested, but she didn't know what to do. She applied for welfare but was turned down because Maury was employed. She started to cry again; she said she loved him but his addiction was hurting the family. I told her to give me a day or two and I would figure something out to help the situation.

That night when I was at home I came up with a solution to Maury Blake's gambling problem. The only issue was that I might have a problem with my job as a probation officer. The next day I met with Bill Pennza, the manager of the health club I owned. Once I took the job as a probation officer, I had to either sell the club or have someone else manage it for me. Bill Pennza was one of my closest friends since high school. Bill was retired from Lincoln Electric Company and was looking for something to do. He took the job as my manager of the health club. Hiring Bill was one of the smartest things I ever did, because he did a better job as a manager than I ever did.

The next day I went to the club and sat down with Penzza. I explained the situation I had with Maury. I told him Johnny Banks was a member at the health club. He happened to be a bookie with a high-class clientele, most of whom were wealthy businessmen. He was one of the nicest members and was always recruiting new members for us. I told Pennza I couldn't become directly involved in this because it could affect my job. But, if Bill could talk to Johnny, explain the problem I was having with Maury Blake, and ask him to meet Maury's wife at the club to see if he could come up with a plan to teach her how to book Maury's bets without Maury knowing about it, I would give Johnny a one-year free membership to the health club.

I told Bill to please tell Johnny I would appreciate any help he could give me. I didn't want to send Maury to prison; he had such a beautiful family, it just didn't make any sense to me. But his gambling was destroying him and his family. The next day Bill called me and told me that Johnny Banks was more than willing to talk with Maury's wife and see what he could do to help her. Johnny also said he didn't want a free membership and that it would be his pleasure to help. Johnny gave Bill a time and date when he could meet Maury's wife at the club.

I called Maury's wife and told her that I wanted her to meet a gentleman at my health club and that he may have a solution to this problem. If he couldn't help, she should contact me again. But, if he could help, I didn't want to know about it.

Bill told me that Johnny and Maury's wife met at the club a number of times. It appeared that they were making a lot of progress with Maury's gambling problem. Bill and I never talked to Johnny about his relationship with Maury's wife; we knew he was only helping her and her family with their financial situation. From that time on, I never had a problem with Maury; and his wife never contacted me again.

One afternoon about six months after Maury went off probation, my secretary called me and said there was a woman in the office who would not identify herself, but she wanted to speak to me. When I went to the waiting room I was surprised to see Maury's wife, looking radiant and like she didn't have a care in the world. I walked to the lobby of the building where we could talk. She told me that she's never been happier, that she had her own car, and they were able to pay off all the restitution owed to the government for the back taxes. They were in the process of buying a home. She wanted to thank me for introducing her to Johnny Banks. Johnny knew Maury's bookie and, somehow, he had convinced the man to let him take over Maury's account. Then, Johnny taught her how to book all of Maury's bets. She said the strange thing was that Maury still didn't know that she was his bookie! She had set up a private bank account and private phone with an answering service just to handle Maury's bets.

The only question I had was how did she pay off a bet when Maury won. She said she gave Johnny Banks the money and he then paid Maury off. Maury thinks he places the bets through Johnny Banks (or his "Secretary" which was really Maury's own wife!). Fortunately, payoffs didn't happen very often. She said, "I pray Maury never finds out. But then, he may not care as long as he can keep on betting!".

## AN UNEXPECTED SURPRISE

One morning, Alvin L. Krenzler, a United States Federal Judge for the Northern District of Ohio, was driving his Harley- Davidson motorcycle from the east side of Cleveland to downtown Cleveland's federal court.

He was going about 50 miles an hour on the freeway when a large red pickup truck pulled into his lane; it was not a safe distance away from the Judge and his motorcycle. The passenger in the truck was chewing tobacco and spit out the open window - right in the judge's face. Dark spit covered his plastic goggles, which could have impaired his vision and possibly caused him to have an accident. The two men in the truck were laughing as they sped away.

The judge immediately called the U.S. Marshalls office and gave them the reason he wanted the two men in the pickup truck brought into his courtroom. He gave them the description of the Ford truck and the license number. He told the Marshalls not to tell them why they were being arrested. The judge instructed the Marshalls to bring the two men into his courtroom and make them sit in the back until the judge was ready to speak to them. The two men sat in the courtroom from 9:30 a.m. until 5 p.m., when the judge called them up to his bench. He said, "You're wondering why I had you picked up and brought to my courtroom." The men said, "Yes, sir." The judge reached down and put on his motorcycle helmet. He said to the men, "Now you know why you're here." The two men looked down at the floor and just said, "Yes, sir." "You almost blinded me and could've caused me to have a serious accident. You could be charged with reckless driving and assault. I could impound your truck and place you in jail with a heavy fine. But, I am going to let you off with just a warning. Behave yourselves and don't pass judgment on people, no matter what they're driving." Both men apologized to the judge and said they would behave themselves from that time on. The judge told the U.S. Marshalls to take the two men back to their truck.

## PERCY DWYER

Percy was sentenced to twenty years for armed bank robbery. Three men robbed a bank in Painesville, Ohio. A pedestrian outside the bank recognized Percy, who was immediately arrested. If Percy had given the names of the other two bank robbers, he would have received a reduced sentence of five years instead of the twenty. Percy would not give the authorities any information on the other two robbers. Consequently, he did 15 years of a 20-year sentence and was out on parole for five years.

Before Percy committed the bank robbery in Painesville he led a very normal life. He was married with a young daughter and was gainfully employed as a shoe salesman; he had no prior arrests and appeared to be just an average citizen.

Percy had been out on parole for two years before he was placed under my supervision. He was 62 years old, living alone in one room at a hotel in Cleveland's inner-city. His only income was a small check he received from County welfare every month. Percy was in poor health and, to add to it, he was a very heavy smoker.

The two years Percy had been out of prison he had not made any friends. He spent most of his time working on his hobby, which was collecting National Geographic magazines. The magazines took up most of the spare space in his room. What was interesting was that he had over 50 years of National Geographic magazines in their exact order and all in mint condition. He told me he read every book from cover to cover. After spending some time with Percy, it was obvious he was a very knowledgeable person, with a fantastic memory. After a time, Percy confided in me that he and his two partners in the bank robbery were only going to rob one bank. Each of the men had a different plan for what he would do with the money they stole. Percy said he was going to use the money as a down payment on a home for his wife and daughter and himself.

After Percy was convicted, his wife and daughter never had any contact with him. When Percy had been in prison for just three months, he received a letter from his wife's attorney stating that she had filed for divorce and full custody of their daughter. Percy did not contest either action. Percy's sister, who lived in Cincinnati, Ohio, tried to communicate with Percy's wife by phone and mail, but to no avail.

As the years went by, Percy's sister was still unable to find out where Percy's wife and daughter were living; she was also unable to locate Percy's wife's parents. It appeared the wife and daughter and parents had disappeared. It was obvious that they wanted nothing to do with Percy or his sister. After a time, Percy came to the realization that he had lost his wife and daughter.

For the first two years of Percy's parole, he was supervised by a different officer. When that officer was relocated, I was appointed to supervise Percy. Percy had been ordered to report into our office once a month. My secretary told me that she remembered Percy. When he came into our offices, his previous supervisor always made him sit and wait for at least a half hour before he saw him. My secretary said she could see Percy was very nervous and embarrassed about being at the office. So the first thing I did was to tell Percy that he did not have to report into the office; I would see him at his residence, and no one in his building would have to know who I was or what our connection was. I think that this helped change our relationship to a more positive nature. I told him I did not want to mail him anything from our office, e.g., setting up appointment dates and times for our meetings. If he would fill me in on his daily schedule, I would meet him at his convenience.

The first meeting that I had with Percy outside of the office was at the old hotel that had been renovated and set up for senior citizens. He had a one-room apartment with a kitchen that had two chairs and a table, a closet, and a small bathroom. Unfortunately, the room had a bad smell. He was aware of this and he apologized; he said he smoked only 10 cigarettes a day because that was all he could afford.

Percy's prison records reflected that he had worked in the prison laundry. The steam and strong bleach had affected his lungs, and he had developed lung cancer. As a result, he lost one of his lungs. I thought it would be better if he stopped smoking entirely, but I didn't say anything at the time. But, it was something that I would work on later, for the sake of his health. When Percy was released from prison at age 62 he was able to obtain Social Security because he had paid into Social Security from age 18 to 47, when he was arrested and sent to prison. His monthly payments were small, but he was able to survive on the limited income.

Percy informed me that three mornings a week from

8 a.m. to 12 noon he did volunteer work at Goodwill Industries at a location that sold used merchandise at a very low cost. People would bring in used furniture, books, clothes, kitchen utensils, TV's, etc. They would receive a form showing the value of the items they gave that could be used as a tax write-off. Percy would do some cleaning and setting up shelves. He said people would drop off books and magazines and, once in a while, he would run into a National Geographic magazine that he was looking for to add to his collection. Percy was of Irish descent and came from a very religious family; he attended St. John's Cathedral in downtown Cleveland. He also spent three mornings a week at the Cleveland public library on Superior Avenue.

Percy told me he was having a problem with his eyes. I told him I had a friend who was a doctor with an office at East Ninth and Euclid and that his prices were very reasonable. A week later I set up an appointment with Dr. Marvin Latter, Percy, and myself at the doctor's office. Before our meeting, I talked to Dr. Latter and told him Percy was a friend of mine with limited income. And, if he would give Percy a break on the cost of the exam and glasses, I would give him a free one-year membership to the downtown health club. Two days later Dr. Latter examined Percy and told me he made up two pairs of glasses, one of which would be sunglasses. A day or so later I was going to give Dr. Latter a membership card to the downtown health club, but he refused the card because Percy had asked him if he could work off the exam and glasses; Dr. Latter was able to find a project for Percy to work off his bill.

Dr. Latter called Percy "The Professor" because he enjoyed all conversations with Percy. They both were interested in the National Geographic magazine. Dr. Latter said he only looked at the pictures and the subtitles, but Percy could tell Dr. Latter word for word about the article that they were talking about.

About six months later, Percy called me at the office and asked if he could stop in at the office and see me. I was so surprised for him to come to the office; I thought that was the last thing he would ever do. Percy informed me he was seeing a woman who was 20 years younger than him. Her name was Gloria Kopanski. She was a librarian at the Cleveland public library; she'd never been married and, in fact, had been a Catholic nun for 15 years. Though she left the convent, she was still very religious and active in her church.

Percy told me about her and their relationship. "It is strange how we became involved. For about a year we occasionally spoke and, one day, I was at her desk and she was talking on the phone to someone in Polish. After she hung up, I said something in Polish and from then on we only spoke to each other in Polish. We started eating lunch together at the library. She told me she lived in a duplex house; she's on one side and her sister and brother-in-law live on the other. The home was in a Polish neighborhood off of East 55th and Broadway in Cleveland. She was very active at St. Stanislaus Catholic Church. She drives and has her own car. About three months after we were seeing each other at the library, she invited me to meet her sister and brother-in-law, who own and operate a travel agency in Cleveland. One day we went out to dinner and then to the Christmas Eve mass and, to my surprise, the mass was in Polish and English. After Christmas, I had to tell her about my past and being in prison. I was terrified she would never speak to me again, but I had to be honest with her because we were getting too close.

"One evening I sat down with Gloria, her sister and her brother-in-law and I told them about being married and having a daughter, the bank robbery, the time in prison and that you were my parole officer for two more years. Gloria's brother-in-law asked how is it that I am Irish and yet speak Polish fluently. I told the three of them that my cellmate in prison was Polish and could hardly speak English. So we made an agreement: for five years, I taught him how to speak English and he taught me how to speak Polish. I was even able to get books to learn to read and write Polish. I really believe that is what kept me from going insane in prison."

Percy asked me if I could meet with Gloria at her home some evening. The reason being that I could confirm everything he told her is true. Percy said he wanted to make sure she knew everything about him so she could trust him to do the right thing if they should get married.

One evening I met Gloria at her home. I found her to be a very warm, intelligent person. After talking with Gloria for over an hour, it was obvious that Percy had told her the truth about his history, not excluding a thing. I told Gloria I trusted Percy and thought that they would make a harmonious couple. I wished them the best of luck.

About a month later, Percy was able to get an annulment from the Catholic Church due to the fact that his wife and daughter had disappeared. Gloria's sister and brother-in-law stood up with them in a small church wedding. The only thing Gloria asked Percy was that he stop smoking because she loved him and wanted to keep him alive and healthy.

A month later I visited Percy and Gloria at Gloria's home. Percy looked like a different person, much healthier and much more personable. He gave his National Geographic magazine collection to a local library. Gloria and Percy were hired by Gloria's sister and brother-in-law at their travel agency. Gloria managed the trips and Percy was the tour guide. Gloria's sister and brother-in-law loved Percy because he was so informative and made every trip a lot more interesting. They could plan trips anywhere in the world because Percy was a natural born tour guide.

I never asked Percy about his two friends who

robbed the bank with him. I thought it would scar our relationship. But I couldn't help wondering what they did with the money they stole. It's been my experience that most bank robbers squander the money, like the old saying "easy come, easy go".

## BETTY RUSCINE

Betty Ruscine was a 60-year old woman who was arrested for cashing a stolen $500 money order.

Betty lived alone in a trailer park, her husband having been killed 20 years before in a traffic accident.. Her only living relative was an older brother who lived in Chattanooga, Tennessee.

On one occasion, her brother James came to visit her. He gave her a postal money order for $500. It turned out that the money order was part of $20,000 in money orders stolen from a Chattanooga post office.

Betty cashed the money order, which the postal inspectors easily traced back to her. When questioned by the postal inspectors, she claimed she didn't know the money order was stolen. She was charged with cashing a stolen postal money order. When she was interrogated by the postal inspectors about where her brother James was, she refused to tell them.

Once a person has been arrested in the Federal Court, it is the job of the Probation Department to interview the defendant and do a presentence report. I was assigned to do the investigation and the presentence report. This consists of doing a complete history on the individual, starting with any prior criminal record, family history, employment background, education, religion, and home address.

Betty had no prior arrests, not even a traffic ticket. She was born and raised in Tennessee; her father had been a coal miner. When Betty was 14 years of age, her father became seriously ill with black lung disease and he was unable to work any more.

Betty completed the 10th grade; in high school she was an excellent student of average intelligence. Unfortunately she had to quit school to go to work to help support the family. She had one older brother who appeared to be very little help in giving family support. He had a number of arrests, mostly for domestic disturbances involving him and his common law wife. The most serious arrests were for driving while intoxicated. It appears he could not hold down a job for very long because he had a problem with alcohol.

Betty had a job with General Electric, where she worked for 19 years and eight months; she had an excellent work record. Betty informed me that she was terrified that she might have to go to prison and she would lose her retirement because you must complete 20 years of employment before receiving any retirement. I checked her employment status and found that what Betty stated was correct. And I made sure that her employment status was in the presentence report. It also should be noted the last thing in the presentence report was the recommendation from the probation officer who did the investigation. This report and recommendation is set up to help the judge in determining the sentence. Usually, the judge will go along with the probation officer's recommendation.

I found out before I made my recommendation that the judge was enraged because Betty would not tell the postal inspectors where her brother was. My recommendation was to place Betty on two years probation and for the first year she would do 10 hours of community service a week. After I submitted my recommendation I went to the judge's office and asked his law clerk if I could talk to the judge to make sure he considered the fact that, if Betty went to prison, she would lose her retirement. The judge's law clerk told me, "You're not going to change the judge's mind; and, on top of that, he may fire you for questioning his decision..."

When Betty was sentenced, the judge did not go along with my recommendation. He sentenced her to two years: the first six months in prison and the remainder of 18 months on probation; she also had to pay restitution of $500. Betty lost her job and her retirement. After I heard what the judge had done, I despised him; when I heard he was retiring, I was thankful he was leaving the court. Then, if there is a hereafter, he will have to answer for his cruel treatment of little people.

## THE JUDGE and MR. ABOUNADER

One evening I was having dinner at the Inn of the Barrister with two friends, Bill Adams and Karl Abounader. Karl, the owner of the Inn told us about his father from Lebanon who had just taken another test for citizenship. He was told if he failed the test three times, he wasn't permitted to take the test again. Unfortunately, this was the third time Mr. Abounader had taken and failed. Karl said his father was so depressed that he kept repeating, "I love America. All I've ever wanted was to be an American citizen."

Bill Adams said to me, "Since you know all the judges, do you think you could talk to one of them to see if there's any chance that Karl's father could re-take the test?".

Karl told us his father had a problem with English, and he would get so nervous when being tested that he couldn't think straight. I met Karl's father a number of times; he was a short, stocky, muscular, hard-working laborer. He never asked anything of this country. He just worked hard and raised a beautiful family.

I told Bill Adams and Karl that Judge Battisti had a soft spot for the underdog, but that I couldn't make any promises. So I asked them not to say anything to Mr. Abounader. I was pretty sure Judge Battisti's parents had come from Italy, so I thought he would understand about Mr. Abounader.

The next week, I went to see Judge Battisti. He was the chief judge who had ruled that the Cleveland public school sytem was guilty of racial segregation. Jack Wohl was the judge's courtroom deputy at the time of the judgement. When Jack was interviewed by the news media, he told them a lot of people hated the judge because he instituted busing as a solution to the racial segregation in the city of Cleveland. Jack also told the news media that the people that hated the judge must not know him, because the people that knew him loved him. I concur.

When I talked with the judge, I told him about Mr. Abounader's problem. The judge told me to bring Mr. Abounader into his office Friday after 3:00 p.m. and he would see what he could do for him.

On Friday, Bill Adams brought Mr. Abounader into the judge's chambers and I met them there. After we walked into the judge's chambers, Jack Wohl introduced Mr. Abounader, Bill and myself to the judge and the two immigration officers. I wasn't expecting immigration officers to be present. I could see that Mr. Abounader was shaking like a leaf, demonstrating that he was a nervous wreck.

The immigration officers sat and waited for the

judge to preside over the hearing. The judge announced to Mr. Abounader and the officers that he would be giving Mr. Abounader an oral test and, if he passed, he would become an American citizen.

The first question the judge asked Mr. Abounader was, "Who was the first president of the United States?" Mr. Abounader answered, "Ronnie Reagan." The judge stated he was going to rephrase the question. "When this country was first started, who was voted in as the president?" Mr. Abounader replied, "George Washington was that man." The judge's second question was, "Who is the president of the United States today?" Mr. Abounader said, "Ronnie Reagan." The judge said, "This is the last question. Take your time and think about what I am saying." Mr. Abounader said, "Yes, sir." "If you are given citizenship and the United Stated went to war, would you fight for this country?" Mr. Abounader jumped up and replied, "I would die for this country! Oh, I love America!" The Judge stood up and said, "You are an American citizen." He pointed to the immigration officers and said, "Do you understand that Mr. Abounader is now an American citizen?"

The immigration officers said they understood. Tearfully, Mr. Abounader thanked the judge and proceeded to pick up the judge and hug him.

Later, I thanked Judge Battisti for what he did. The judge replied, "It was my pleasure; it made my day!"

# HENRY CARTER

When I was a probation officer, I had a probationer named Henry Carter. He and his wife Carrie were charged with receiving a U.S. government tax refund check but claiming they had never received it. They received another check in the same amount to replace the missing check. But a short time later, the original check was found and it was proven that the Carters had, in fact, signed and cashed that original check. They were charged and sentenced to two years probation and they had to repay the government the money they used from the second check, which was a little over four hundred dollars.

Henry appeared to have lower than average intelligence, but he received a break in his rent by doing odd jobs for his landlord. Unfortunately, Henry had a rare skin disorder that was not contagious, but his face and arms were so afflicted that it made him look repulsive. In addition, he had very strong body odor. Because of his looks and odor, Henry had a very difficult time finding employment.

Henry's wife Carrie also appeared to have a lower than average intelligence. Her hair was always a mess and had three different colors to it; she only had three teeth in her mouth. I told Henry to take his wife to the Case Western Reserve Dental School. I had known three people that received free treatment at the school, and there was a good chance that, if he took his wife there, she could obtain free dentures. Unfortunately, this never happened.

Henry's son Jason was nine years old and he also appeared slow. But he was in the fourth grade at the local school, which was the right grade for his age.

On one cold winter day, I visited the Carters' apartment and, when I walked in, I was shocked by the awful smell. I noticed a large number of bags of garbage on the kitchen floor, so I questioned Henry, asking him what were all those bags doing there when he had free City garbage collection. Henry told me the bags give off heat, and their gas heater wasn't running since the City turned off their gas because they were three months behind in payment.

I said, "You're on welfare. Why didn't you pay the bill?". Henry told me they needed the money for other things. I noticed he and his wife were both drinking beer, so I questioned him about using their welfare check to buy beer instead of food. His wife spoke up and said, "We buy food with our food stamps." Henry claimed he did not buy beer with their welfare check. He said he only used the money he earned from doing odd jobs in the neighborhood for their beer money. He said, if they didn't have to pay the government back for the second check they cashed, they would be able to pay their gas bill. What a mess!

With the help of my union friends, I was able to obtain a job for Henry as a garbage collector in one of

Cleveland's suburbs. Henry was thrilled, and his life changed drastically. He bought his son a puppy and a two-wheel bike; he bought a kitchen set and a small TV for the apartment.

Unfortunately, the situation did not last.

Henry had only worked eight weeks when the City fired him, saying he was physically unable to do the work. The truth was that his coworkers did not want to work with him because of his appearance and smell. The workers said they were going to strike unless the City got rid of Henry.

Later, Henry tried to get unemployment benefits, but a person had to have worked twenty weeks in order to draw unemployment. So Henry was shot down and had to go back on welfare.

Three months later, the Carters were in trouble with the government again. Henry had received his income tax return check. He was able to get back everything he had paid in to IRS because he had only worked eight weeks that year. I couldn't believe what happened next.

The Carters, once again, claimed they had lost their refund check and they requested another one. The Feds immediately investigated the Carters' claim and learned they had gone to a check-cashing establishment two blocks from their house to cash the check. The check-cashing establishment had taken their pictures when they cashed the check they claimed was lost.

The Carters were in trouble again with the court.

This time they were being charged with a probation violation. I had to submit a recommendation to the court; I recommended that the Carters be severely reprimanded and told that, if the court has a problem with them again, they would be sent to prison and their son would have to be placed in a foster home.

When the Feds found out about my recommendation, they were upset. They informed the Judge that they felt my recommendation was too lenient and that the Carter's should be sent to prison. The Judge called the two agents and me into his office; he asked me if I could justify my recommendation. I gave the judge and the two agents the Carters' history while on probation. I further stated that having the Carter's sent to prison was not the answer. I was told that it costs the government eighty thousand dollars a year to house an inmate. I said I think we should continue to try to find some type of employment for the Carter's because they are so handicapped.

The judge looked at the two agents and said the court would "...follow Bill's recommendation". It was so rewarding to work with a Judge who was willing to look at the extenuating circumstances in this case.

Shortly after that incident, I retired. But I continue to wonder how the Carters are getting along.

# MR. POLASKI

Mr. Polaski lived with his brother and sister in the inner city on the east side of Cleveland. All of them were retired after having worked in a large company three blocks from their home. The presentence report indicated that the company they had worked for closed down or had relocated.

Mr. Polaski ruled the family with an iron fist; he made all the decisions for the three of them. The family belonged to the local Catholic parish, where the sister had been very active in church functions. However, after the family stopped working, they also stopped going to church. Evidently, they just stayed inside the house since the neighborhood had become too dangerous for them to be out walking unless it was to buy necessities.

They also had a three-legged dog that was almost blind and very feeble.

Mr. Polaski was under probation supervision for three years and I was assigned to his case for the entire time. He had been charged with income tax evasion. His sentence was three years probation, a fine, and he had to pay the balance of the taxes owed.

When I would make a house visit, it was obvious that Mr. Polaski resented me being there even though he knew it was one of the conditions of his probation that I would see him at home once a month. Mr. Polaski was the only one who talked to me. I thought maybe the brother and sister could not speak English, I knew they spoke Polish.

In the home, there was a twelve-inch black and white TV and the furniture was in an impossible state of repair. I felt the house could have been on one of those programs showing the family to be hoarders. The front porch had so much junk on it that you could hardly get to the front door, and the inside was almost as bad. They had lived in the same house for almost forty years.

I checked on Mr. Polaskis' financial situation. Even though he had to pay a large fine and back taxes, the family's bank account was well over $200,000. Moreover, all three of the Polaski's were over sixty-two years of age, so they could receive retirement and Social Security benefits.

I was appalled at the way the family was living. I told Mr. Polaski there was no reason to live in a neighborhood with such a high crime rate in a rat infested part of the inner city.

The next time I visited Mr. Polaski's house, I told him that living here could be a violation of his probation and that he was subjecting his family to a dangerous and unhealthy situation. I also said that, if I notified the judge, he might be cited as a probation violator and sent to prison.

I told Mr. Polaski that I had checked his financial status and that his family should buy a home in a nice neighborhood. None of them drove, so I told him to make sure the home was close to a shopping center and a Catholic church.

I also said that their dog was so old and sickly that they should take the dog to a veterinarian and see if the vet could help it. Unfortunately, the veterinarian determined that the dog was in such a poor state of physical and mental health that it had to be put to sleep.

It was obvious that Mr. Polaski hated me. But, he did as I instructed him to do. He found a nice three-bedroom brick home in a middle-class neighorhood about a block away from a Catholic church and an adequate shopping center.

After they moved to the new location, I stopped in to check on them. I was about to leave when Mr. Polaski's sister came outside the house and handed me a cake she had just baked. She said, in English, "Thank you for being our guardian angel." That's when I knew I had done the right thing.

## FRED PUTZ

When I still owned the downtown health club, I took a job as a probation and parole officer. This meant I had to hire a manager for the health club, so I hired my close friend Bill Pennza. Bill did a great job and, in fact, more than earned his pay, because he was better at collecting membership dues than I ever was.

One of the parolees I was supposed to supervise, I'll call him Fred Putz to protect the guilty, was a real thorn in my side. When Fred was in prison, he worked in the prison boiler room. One of the boilers sprang a pinhole leak and the steam pressure spurting from that hole cut off Fred Putz's hand. As a result, he was given a prosthesis. It was a metal hook that opened and closed when Fred rotated his arm.

After Fred was paroled from prison, he had to stay in a halfway house in Cleveland. He was instructed to report to my office because he had some unique problems that had to be handled. He said he had a problem with the IRS and the state tax department. He told me he and his partner owned a bar, which the partner operated while Fred was incarcerated.

His partner may have managed the bar, but he didn't bother to pay any federal or state taxes during the time Fred was otherwise occupied. To top it off, Fred's partner had disappeared before Fred was released from prison. So, Fred was charged with failing to pay his back taxes. He asked me if I would talk to the IRS and the state and, maybe, get an offer in compromise. I was able to talk to the IRS and the state tax department and get all charges dropped. Working this out with the tax departments was going above and beyond the call of duty for my position as a parole officer.

After everything was cleared up, Fred came to see me the next day. He said, "Since you were able to clear the charges against me with the state and IRS, maybe you could help me find a job." As luck would have it, I had a few good contacts and I was able to get Fred a job as a janitor in a social service agency.

Fred came to me with his next problem. He said he still didn't have a place to live. So I talked to two lawyers who were members of my health club; they both worked for Metropolitan Housing in Cleveland. They were able to get Fred a small apartment on the near west side of Cleveland. It was little, but it was low income housing, which would also help Fred in his financial situation.

A short time later, Fred was arrested and placed in the county jail. He was under investigation because his girlfriend was found dead in his apartment. I was able to check out the girlfriend's medical history, which indicated she had several attempts at suicide. So I informed the court of this fact. Later I heard that the case was ruled a suicide and Fred was released.

While Fred was still in the local jail, an ex-probationer who had been in jail with Fred came into my office. He told me while he was in on a misdemeanor delinquency parking ticket charge, he heard Fred Putz was telling anybody that would listen that his parole officer was a no-good son of a bitch and a real prick. Of course, Fred named me as his parole officer. Fred said I was always nosing into his life and picking on him.

I was shocked at what the ex-probationer said. But I thought maybe there were hard feelings between him and Fred and maybe he was trying to get Fred into trouble, so I tried to forget what the guy said.

A day or so later, an old friend named Eric Hall, who was a retired East Cleveland police officer, called me. He told me his son worked at the county jail as a guard. Eric said his son told him there was a prisoner named Fred Putz in custody and that this prisoner was saying nasty things about his parole officer – who turned out to be me. Eric immediately called me and told me about Fred Putz and that the things he was saying about me were not nice. Eric's son stated that he thought Fred Putz was a big bull shitter and that I should have a good talk with him.

The next day I called Fred into my office to confront him with what I had heard. Fred stood up and said, "If you weren't here with all your parole officer buddies, I would kick your ass!" I told Fred he could leave and I would see him later. When Fred left my office and went to the elevators, I immediately ran down the back steps and out of the building. When Fred came around the corner of the building, I grabbed him and threw him against the wall. I said, "It's just you and me, Fred. So start swinging because I'm going to shove that hook right up your ass!". Fred stepped back and folded his arms and said, "Mr. Bayles, you've lost complete control of yourself."

He was right, and I walked back to my office. I never mentioned the incident to anyone. Fred Putz never apologized or said he was sorry for the things he said. I thought maybe he hated me because he had to ask for help. He finished his parole time with no more incidents. In fact, the few times I saw him on the street, he would turn the other way or cross the street to avoid contact with me.

## INSTITUTIONALIZED

In reading the life history of Timothy Marinelli, I couldn't figure out why in the world he would become a criminal. He appeared to be living a normal prosperous life.

He graduated from high school, completed four years in the United States Navy with an honorable discharge, and then married his high school sweetheart who was the prom queen at their high school. He acquired a job as a fabricator in a large company in the Cleveland area. After getting married, they had two healthy sons and purchased a home in a middle-class neighborhood.

Tim's best friend was Ronald Curtis. Ronald's father owned a hunting cabin in the West Virginia mountains. When Ronald and Tim were in high school, Ronald's father took them to West Virginia and taught them how to hunt. So every year after that, Tim, Ronald and his father would spend several weekends a year hunting in West Virginia.

Tim and Ronald joined the U.S. Navy on the same day, thinking they would be together in the Navy. But, as it turned out, Tim was stationed in Norfolk, Virginia and Ronald was stationed in San Diego, California. Before Ronald went into the service he was dating a girl from high school and they planned to marry. Ronald sent all his Navy pay to his girlfriend. Unfortunately, while he was in the service, she fell in love with another person. The girlfriend married that person and moved out of the state. She kept Ronald's money. Ronald was bitter and he never married; as far as I know he still lives with his parents.

Tim's leisure activities included: hunting, fishing, and listening to hard rock music. He also had a hobby making things out of sheet metal. Some of the things he made were very artistic; e.g., bird cages, bread boxes, hanging lanterns. Some of the other things he made were a bobsled and a tree-stand for hunting in West Virginia. Tim came up with an idea to build a metal insert that would fit into a large street mailbox so that, in case the box was damaged and the door could not be opened, a postal person could recover the mail that was stuck in the damaged box. He was able to patent this idea but, unfortunately, the post office turned down his proposal.

Tim was arrested for using his mailbox insert equipment. By placing the insert in the bank's night deposit box and waiting until the venue had finished the concert and made their night deposit, Tim would return later and withdraw the insert, which would have all the money that was deposited for that evening. For example, Blossom Music Center in Cuyahoga Falls, Ohio, could have over 13,000 people in attendance at a concert and average $50 a ticket; if only half the people paid cash that night, the night deposit would be about $32,000. If Tim robbed three banks using his night deposit box insert, his "take" was well over $100,000 for a good night's work. After the second bank was robbed, the Feds figured the robber was following the hard rock performers from one venue to another. The Feds were waiting at the third concert and watched the banks in the area. They saw Tim place his insert in the night deposit box at the bank and then, when Tim later withdrew the insert containing the contents of the deposit, he was arrested and charged with three bank robberies.

Even though most of the money was recovered, Tim was sentenced to eight years in prison; he spent the next four years in a minimum security prison and then was released on parole to finish out the final four years. Tim spent the next few months in a halfway house, until his wife permitted him to come home. I was able to convince a good friend, Tony Liberatore, who was head of the Cement Laborers Union, to give Tim a job as a flag waver for a large construction company. Tim was short and very slender and would not be capable of doing any heavy labor.

Tim did not appear to be too happy with his home life. His wife had become active in the Jehovah's Witnesses church, which Tim had no interest in. His two sons showed no interest in playing or watching sports; the boys liked sitting around playing video games. On one of my visits to Tim's home, he told me, "The only love I get out of this house is from my hunting dog, and we can't go hunting because I'm not allowed to own a gun."

Tim spent most of his time with his friend Ronald because they both had the same interests: attending hard rock concerts, going to sporting events such as the Cleveland Browns, the Indians, and the Cavaliers. He and his wife had very little in common anymore so they spent very little time together.

In the early spring when Tim was laid off he told his wife he was going with Ron and his father to their hunting cabin in West Virginia. He said, even though he could not hunt, he would enjoy hanging out with them.

Tim did not request permission to go out of state. This made him a parole violator and he could be sent back to prison to finish out the balance of his sentence. The records reflect that Tim had no intention of going to the hunting cabin. Instead, he went back to the thing he was arrested for originally: bank robbery. This time Tim did not follow all the rock stars from place to place. What he did instead was pick the most popular rock stars and rob the park where they performed before the largest audience on their tour. This would give him a large pay off. The Feds figured that, in the six months that Tim was active in his bank robbery expedition, he had accumulated over a million dollars.

After a big rock concert in Los Angeles, California, Tim had placed his insert equipment in a night deposit box in which the park had deposited over $60,000. For some unknown reason, Tim did not go back to collect his insert equipment, so the money that was in the night deposit box remained there. The next day that the bank was open, they saw that the bank deposit box could not be emptied. The authorities were contacted and the Feds were able to withdraw Tim's equipment and give the contents to the bank.

From that time on, there was no record of any night depositories being robbed. Three months later, Tim came back to Ohio and turned himself in to the federal authorities. He told the Feds that he was living in a condominium in Las Vegas, Nevada and that, three days before he returned to Ohio, his condominium had been robbed. He told the Feds that he was at a show at one of the casinos and it was a stormy night when the robbers broke into his condominium. They not only took his personal belongings, but they stole a large TV, a microwave oven and a lamp. He immediately called the

Las Vegas police and the police report revealed that Tim's condominium had been broken into and that there were at least two or more people involved in the break-in. When Tim was arrested he only had $40 on him and, in searching his car, the Feds found nothing.

When I interviewed Tim, he apologized for what he did and thanked me for trying to help him by getting him a job so he could get back with his family. I questioned him about what would happen to his wife and sons. He said they'd be fine and wouldn't even miss him. He said his parents and her parents would be there for his family if help were needed. And then he said something strange: "Believe me. I know for a fact that they will be well taken care of.". That made me very suspicious; I was thinking maybe Tim knew where the money was hidden or someone who Tim could trust had the money.

Prison records reflect that none of his family came to visit him. The only visitor he had was his friend Ronald Curtis. The Feds did not entirely believe Tim's story about being robbed and they investigated Tim's family, his relatives, and even Ronald Curtis. But, after interviewing them, it was obvious that they knew nothing about the million dollars that had disappeared.

Tim did not seem a bit troubled that he was going to prison for a long time. He told me he would read sports magazines and watch sporting events on TV. He said, "I won't have any worries. I'll get three meals a day, a warm place to sleep. What more can a person ask for?"

The Feds and I both thought that Tim didn't lose the money. But, then again, I can't stop wondering where the money is.

When I saw the movie "Shawshank Redemption" that starred Morgan Freeman, he described an institutionalized person that clearly described Tim Marinelli.

## TWO BROTHERS

This story is about two brothers, Mike and Marty Paycheck. Mike was born in Yugoslavia; his parents brought him to the United States when he was five years old. Marty was born here in the United States. The two boys did not look like brothers: Mike was a large muscular man who was very personable and always the life of the party; Marty was short and thin and very quiet. It was obvious that Marty idolized Mike.

When Mike was 24 and Marty was 18, they were arrested in Florida by the US Coast Guard for trying to smuggle a boatload of marijuana into this country from Mexico. They were tried in a federal court and sentenced to five years in prison. They were paroled after serving one year. Mike was married at the time, with three children. Mike's parents took the wife, Carol, and the three children to live with them during the year that Mike and Marty were in prison.

When Mike was released from prison, he was able to obtain a job with a large plumbing supply company. Then he purchased a duplex home in the inner-city, on the same street where his parents lived. Marty wasn't as lucky, even though he had gone to a trade school in Cleveland and learned to be an excellent mechanic. Marty married a year after he was released from prison. A year later, he and his wife had twins, a boy and a girl.

AJ was both Mike and Marty's parole officer. (We called him AJ because he had very long first and last names that were very difficult to pronounce.)

Mike let Marty and his family live in the duplex rent-free until Marty could find a full time job. A short time later, Marty found a job as a mechanic at a small used car lot. Unfortunately, the owner of the car lot was not a decent person; he tried to talk Marty into changing the odometers on the used cars, which would make the cars easier to sell because of having low mileage. Marty told the owner he wouldn't touch the odometers because he didn't want to go back to prison. The owner was always lying to his customers, saying things like "This is a one-owner car and the person took excellent care of the car." He charged the highest interest rate possible and, if the buyer was a day late making his payment, the owner would garnishee the man's wages. The owner was always late paying Marty's wages. Once when the owner was two weeks behind in paying Marty, Marty went to his boss with his wife and two kids. He said, "This is my family. They need to eat. So please pay me.". The owner gave Marty a check; but, when Marty went to cash it, the check bounced.

Marty told Mike what the owner of the car lot was doing to him. Mike told Marty to come with him to see the car lot owner and said he'd make sure that Marty would get paid. When Mike and Marty got to the car lot, Mike told the car lot owner, "No more checks. Cash right now." Then, Mike pulled out a gun and pointed it at the car lot owner. Just then a Cleveland policeman came into the building and saw Mike pointing the gun at the car lot owner. The policeman pulled his gun and yelled for Mike to drop his gun. Mike turned and was pointing the gun at the policeman, who shot Mike and hit him in the heart. He died instantly. Marty was hysterical, screaming at the policemen, "We were not robbing this man. We were only trying to get the money that he owed me!" The policeman immediately picked up the gun and, when he checked the gun, there were no bullets in it.

After this incident at the car dealer's office, AJ was told by his supervisor that he had to contact the parole board and cite Marty as a parole violator because Marty was involved in the commission of a crime and also that AJ should recommend Marty be sent back to prison.

AJ and I talked about this case and we both agreed Marty had been punished enough for God's sake. Marty lost his brother. We both felt the car lot owner should be punished, not Marty. AJ contacted the parole commission but did not recommend that that Marty be sent back to prison. He explained to the commission the circumstances that ended up with Mike pointing the gun at the car dealer. He also stated that Marty did not know Mike had a gun. In fact, Marty remembered that Mike had given two guns to his father because a condition of his parole was that he could not own a gun. The police report stated that the gun was not loaded and that all Mike wanted to do was to scare the car dealer into paying Marty the wages he was owed. AJ also noted that Marty was needed at home. He would have to take care of two families now that Mike was dead.

AJ and I talked to Tony Liberatore, president of the Cement Laborers Union. Tony had been very helpful in finding employment for ex-convicts. We asked Tony if he could get Marty a job in the union. Tony said Marty was too small for construction work and, besides that, he was a trained mechanic. So Tony gave AJ the name of the owner of a Ford car dealership. "Tell him Tony Liberatore sent you and explain Marty's problem." AJ did as he was instructed and the car dealer thanked Tony for sending Marty to him. He said Marty was an excellent mechanic and very dependable.

AJ went to the Better Business Bureau about the car lot owner and told them about how he was trying to get Marty to reset the odometers. Unfortunately, it was the car lot owner's word against Marty's.

The policeman that shot Mike was following proper procedures in this incident. But the policeman's wife said her husband was very depressed and she wanted him to quit the force. She was afraid that, next time someone aimed a gun at him, he wouldn't shoot. The policeman stated, "Right or wrong, I killed an innocent man and I'll never forget it."

Thank God Marty had AJ as his parole officer. I haven't seen many parole officers that would go the extra mile to help their parolees. Marty made an excellent adjustment. He loves his work and has good pay with benefits. He and his parents are taking care of Mike's family.

## A TEA PARTY

In the 1970's Cleveland was called the bombing capital of the United States. There were 21 bombings in the Cleveland area. All the bombings resulted from an altercation between the Cleveland mafia and the Irish mob leader Danny Greene and a union boss named John Nardi. As best I can recall, this war started when there was a fallout over money that Danny Greene owed Shonder Birns, who was a notorious rackets figure and a close associate of the Cleveland mafia.

Because Danny Greene refused to pay Shonder,

Shonder made an attempt to bomb Danny Greene's car. But, somehow, the bomb exploded without injuring Danny Greene. Once Danny Greene knew Shonder was after him, he, in turn, put a bomb under Shonder Birns' car. It exploded and killed Shonder instantly. After that incident the Cleveland mafia retaliated by killing John Nardi with a bomb.

Eugene Ciasullo was a boyhood friend and we kept in touch until his death. A few years after high school, I heard that Eugene was a notorious mafia enforcer. Eugene and I saw each other quite frequently over the years. I have to tell my readers that Eugene never asked me to do anything illegal, immoral, or improper. He was a good friend and I was lucky to call him a friend.

As one of my side jobs, I owned a small men's' health club in downtown Cleveland. Eugene was a member and at times he would bring in guests. Two of his guests were mafia soldiers that were under Eugene's command. One was Allie Calabrese and the other was Pasqual "Butchie" Cisternino. The only thing I remember about Butchie was that he was a quiet, friendly person. In 1976 a bomb was placed in a flowerpot at Eugene Ciasullo's Richmond Heights home. The bomb exploded as he walked by. It was figured that the bomb was placed by one of Danny Greene's mob members. Eugene was seriously injured by metal and glass puncturing his intestines.

As soon as I heard Eugene was injured I went to the hospital. When I got to Eugene's room, I was happy to find him coherent and alert. We shook hands and I said, "What's going on? It's obvious that there are people out there trying to kill you. And there is no one here to protect you." Eugene said, "See that good looking priest out in the hall? Well, he's no priest." Then Eugene threw back his covers to show me two guns lying next to him. Eugene didn't spend too much time in the hospital. I was amazed how fast he recovered. He was one tough guy.

The Cleveland mafia found out that Danny Greene was an FBI informant. But that wasn't the reason they wanted him dead. It was because he was trying to take over the Cleveland mafia's illegal operations and because he killed Shonder Birns, who was a close associate of the Cleveland mafia. The FBI had little use for Danny Greene once he became a known informant.

A few years later, after numerous bombing attempts, the Cleveland mafia leader James Licavoli (also known as Jack White) decided they would kill Danny Greene. It was my understanding that Eugene Ciasullo told Jack White the Feds were looking to use Danny Greene one more time by catching them assassinating Greene. Eugene told White that the smart thing to do was to hire an outside contractor so that none of his people would be charged with the crime. Jack White disagreed with Eugene. So Eugene took his family and moved to Florida so that he would not be charged or connected with the killing of Danny Greene.

Jack White should have listened to Eugene. Eugene was right. The Federal Agents arrested so many Cleveland mafia figures in connection with the killing of Danny Greene, it marked the downfall of organized crime in Cleveland Ohio.

One of the people that was charged and convicted in the killing of Danny Greene was Butchie Cisternino, Eugene's friend and associate. In 1986 I was placed in charge of Butchie Cisternino's father, who had a long history of arrests and was convicted for illegal gambling. On my first visit to the parents' home, I told them Mr. Cisternino would not have to come in to the office to turn in his monthly report. I said I would stop at the house and pick up the report. I felt it would save him the headache of having to come all the way into Cleveland. As his probation officer, I not only had to get his report but I had to see him in person.

For the months that followed when I would visit the parents' home, they were unfriendly and very cold. They would come to the door, hand me the report form, and say, "Anything else?" I would say no and they would slam the door in my face. A few months later when I went to visit their home, they opened the door and said, "Come on in Mr. Bayles." They had me sit down at the table with a pot of tea and some oatmeal cookies, I was shocked by this new type of behavior. I told them, "I could understand you slamming the door in my face and treating me like dirt. But this new type of treatment you're giving me is a shock." I asked what was going on. Both parents laughed and said they had visited Butchie in prison and told him I was his dad's probation officer. Butchie told them, "Be good to Bill; he is a nice guy." From that time on, whenever I visited Butchie's parents' home, they presented me with tea and oatmeal cookies and they were very friendly. One thing I always wondered about was how did they know I liked tea and oatmeal cookies.

My friend Eugene Ciasullo retired in 1985 and lived with his family in a suburb of Pittsburgh, Pennsylvnia until his death from natural causes on August 6, 2016.

## A GOOD NEIGHBOR

Willie Waters was arrested twice for receiving and selling stolen goods. The first time he was arrested for selling stolen TVs. A man he met who had robbed an interstate shipment of 36" TVs told Willie they would sell in the store for over $300 but Willie could sell them for $100 and keep $25 for himself. The man would keep the balance.

Willie was able to sell 15 of the TVs to friends and relatives in the neighborhood. When his wife found out what he was doing, she called the authorities and turned Willie in for selling stolen goods. But, when she found out that he might go to prison, she made a deal with the federal agents. She gave them the name of the man who had robbed the shipment of TVs in the first place. She also provided the names of the people that Willie sold the stolen TVs to. As a result of her cooperation, Willie did not have to go to prison. But he was placed on federal probation for three years.

Willie was so furious with his wife for giving information to the federal authorities that he divorced her a few months later. In an interview later, Willie said he divorced his wife because she had hurt so many people, especially friends and relatives. He also said, "She's just too good for me."

Willie was a very likeable person. He was an exceptional handyman, very knowledgeable in doing almost anything; plumbing, carpentry, electrical. He had many friends who would call on him if they had a problem. Most of the time he never got paid, just a lot of promises.

For the next two years Willie adhered to all the conditions of his probation. But at the start of the third year he was introduced to a man selling tires that would sell in stores for $80 to $100. Willie bought 20 tires from the individual for $10 each. Once again Willie started selling stolen property for $20 each. He gave the tires to friends who promised to pay him later when they had the money. Unfortunately, Willie was arrested for selling stolen property. He was unable to give the name of the person he bought the tires from. Willie was charged with receiving stolen property and was cited as a probation violator and sentenced to three years in prison.

After Willie served a year in prison, he was released on parole for two years. I was assigned as his parole officer. He was able to live with his sister, who lived alone and had an extra bedroom for Willie. The apartment was located in Cleveland's inner city.

Because Willie had an excellent reputation as a handyman, he was able to acquire a job with a large apartment complex in the inner city. The owners of the apartment complex knew that he was on parole, but they still hired him for a 40-hour work week with excellent pay.

Because I did not like to drive in rush hour traffic, I stopped at Cleveland State to get a workout before I left for home. I found a partner and played three games of handball. When I finished, I decided I would stop at Willie and his sister's apartment. I hoped to find him and have them fill out his mandatory weekly progress report. It was about 6:30 in the evening, dark, very cold, with a lot of snow on the ground. When I went to the apartment and knocked on the door, I found that no one was home. So I wrote a note saying that I must have the report in my office by Monday or I would have to cite him as a parole violator and he might go back to prison.

When I turned to leave the apartment there were three men blocking the exit door. One man was pointing a gun at me. The other two had their hands in their pockets like they also had guns. The man with the gun said to me, "Your money or your life.". I said, "Okay. Please just stay calm. I have $40 in my pocket. If it's okay, I'll just reach in my pocket and take out the money.". The man with the gun told me to move slowly and drop the money on the floor. I did just as ordered. Then the man told me to backup; again, I obeyed. One of the men picked up the money. Then all three turned around with their backs to me and walked out the exit.

I reached in my coat and pulled out my service revolver. With the gun in my hand I thought, "Am I possibly going to kill these three men for $40? And what am I going to have to go through to explain the situation, not only to my superiors but also to the news media?" I put my gun in my holster and decided not to report the incident.

The following Monday morning Willie came into my office with his parole progress report. I told him about my visit to his apartment Friday evening. Immediately, Willie pulled $40 out of his pocket. I refused it, saying, "I learned a hard lesson. I should not have been there after work hours and without a backup."

I prayed that Willie learned his lesson and never again dealt in stolen merchandise.

# EUGENE CIASULLO

Eugene Ciasullo and I had been friends since high school. Eugene had become a notorious mafia enforcer, but we remained friends over the years, until his recent death. Eugene never asked me to do anything illegal, immoral, or improper.

When Eugene found out that I had taken the job in law enforcement, he told me, "Your boss is a real prick and he can't be trusted. If you ever have a problem with him, let me know. I can straighten him out because we own him. Whenever he did the mob a favor, we have paid him off with money and broads. "

After working at this job for a few years, I had an altercation with my boss. He told me to change a recommendation to the court for one of our prisoners.

I felt that this action was unfair and improper, as this individual was a very young, smalltime dealer just newly on the scene. My boss wanted me to ask for him to be given the same sentence as the biggest, most established dealer in our area of Ohio.

When my boss found out that I would not change my recommendation, he came into my office with my supervisor and started yelling and threatening me.

He said he would have me fired unless I did as he instructed. I told him, "Get out of my office you mafia connected son of a bitch, or I'll kick your ass!"

My boss's face turned white and he ran out of my office, because he now knew I knew who and what he was. At that point my supervisor said to me, "Bill, you're history." I told him, "I'm going to be here long after you and our boss have retired." And that is actually what happened.

# ABOUT THE AUTHOR

Bill Bayles graduated from Shaw High School in East Cleveland, Ohio in 1950. He went on to attend U.S. Navy Corpsman School in Portsmouth, Virginia, graduating in 1953. He then attended Kent State University in Kent, Ohio, from which he received a B.S. degree in 1958, and from 1959-1960 he attended Oberlin College in Oberlin, Ohio to obtain Y.M.C.A. Executive Certification and to study Comparative Religion and World Religions.

In 1970, Bayles achieved a Masters Degree in Physical Education from Case Western Reserve University in Cleveland, Ohio. He then achieved a certification to work in the criminal justice program from Cleveland State University in 1972. Through state college courses, he met the state requirements to become certified to work at the Lorain County Board of Developmental Disabilities.

Bayles worked at the East Cleveland Y.M.C.A. and Y.M.C.A. camp while still in high school. From April 15 to December 8 of 1949, he dropped out of school for one semester to work on a ship on the Great Lakes as a deck hand before graduating in 1950.

From 1951 to 1954, he served as a U.S. Navy Corpsman doing neuropsychiatric services at the Portsmouth Naval Hospital in Virginia. From 1954 to 1958, he worked at the Akron Y.M.C.A. in Akron, Ohio as aquatic director, while also attending school at Kent State University. In the summer of 1956, he worked as the Medina Y.M.C.A. camp director. From 1958 to 1964 he worked at the Cleveland Central Y.M.C.A. as assistant physical director and then director of the youth program, in the main building, outpost, and camp.

From 1964 to 1980, Bayles owned and operated the Downtown Health Club in the Hippodrome Building at 720 Euclid Ave, Cleveland, Ohio. From June 1 of 1965 to September 7 of 1980, he also worked as pool manager at the Beechmont Country Club in Beechwood, Ohio. During the same time, from 1970 to 1980, he worked at Cleveland State University as aquatic director, at the time of which he set up a course called Physical Fitness Orientation. From 1972 until 1998, Bayles taught physical fitness including a course called Leisure in Our Society. In 1988, he and Jerry Friedlander built and ran a health club, the Downtown Fitness Center, in the Leader building in downtown Cleveland. From 1972 until 1992, Bayles was also a U.S. probation and parole officer in the Western District of Ohio. He retired in August of 1992. From 1995 to 1998, Bayles worked as a recreation instructor for the Lorain County Board of Mental Retardation and Developmental Disabilities until he had to retire because he was injured on the job.

Today, he divides his time between California, Florida, and Ohio.

The authors children:

Linda Blum graduated with her bachelor's degree from The Ohio State University and earned her Masters from Youngstown State in social work. She is hired by the court to supervise sex offenders, she has two children and two grandchildren, and her husband Paul is a high school teacher.

Rick Bayles is a Constable in Pennsylvania. He is married to Kathy, a union road worker and they have four children and four grandchildren. His hobbies include hunting and collecting animal hides for his trophy room.

Diane lives on the West Coast with her two children.

Lisa Darone is a registered nurse, and she lives with her companion Ron Denham, a recreation specialist. She has four children and 14 grandchildren and one great grandson. Her hobbies include camping with family and friends and fishing.

David Bayles is a maintenance engineer for a local court, and lives with his wife Judy, retired. They have three children and four grandchildren. His hobbies are fishing, and cooking the fish for friends and family, and writing. He has written numerous "letters to the editor" that have been published in the local newspaper.

Lee Ann Bayles has two college degrees, a registered nurse, and a dental hygienist, but her true talent is interior design. She has two sons. Her hobbies include decorating and traveling.

Michelle Presler is a registered nurse, and lives with her husband Ken, a heating and air-conditioning specialist

She has two children. Michelle hobbies are camping with family and friends and sewing.

Brent Bayles is severely developmentally delayed as a result of an accident when his mother was seven months pregnant. He lives in a group home for medically complicated developmentally delayed individuals.

Dana Bayles is an a occupational therapist, and team lead at a local Outpatient clinic. She lives with her two sons. Her hobbies include camping and traveling.

Jessica Bauer is a graduate of Ohio University with a degree in journalism. She is married to Bill who is a Salesman and they have 4 children. Jessica is a housewife who is very busy raising their children. Jessica likes to make scrap books.

Made in the USA
Middletown, DE
16 April 2018